T0033000

"Difficult. Impossible. Agonizing. All-[...] know is experiencing physical, emotior[...] is for you. It will answer your questions, acknowledge your anguish, deepen your walk with God, assist in understanding the power of scars, and place you on a path of acceptance and healing. In Dr. Michelle Bengtson's book *Sacred Scars*, you'll find comfort and encouragement for your hard journey. This is also a book you will want to purchase for friends who need hope."

Carol Kent, executive director of Speak Up Ministries, speaker, and author of *When I Lay My Isaac Down*

"Pain. We all experience it emotionally, physically, relationally, and even spiritually. While we wish for a pain-free life, the dark seasons are where God invites us into the most growth. In the pages of this book, you will come to understand how God uses pain in powerful ways. If you're human, you need this book."

Jill Savage, host of the *No More Perfect Podcast* and author of *No More Perfect Marriages*

"If you've been wounded and need a reminder that you're not disqualified because of your pain, this book is for you. In *Sacred Scars*, Dr. Bengtson combines her expertise in relationships with her knowledge of the Word of God to offer encouragement and hope. The scars that trigger pain can be reframed to reveal something sacred."

Ashley Elliott, MS, LMHCA, counselor, speaker, and coauthor of *I Used to Be ___*

"Since meeting Dr. Michelle Bengtson, I knew I had to go and devour her work. She carries a mighty stick of dynamite-packaged knowledge and truth through her books, and *Sacred Scars* is no different. It ministered to me in the deepest parts of my soul. I would very much like to sit with my younger self and read *Sacred Scars* to little Rachel. I would tell her that her scars will not be in vain, that God will make something beautiful out of them. This book helped me in my continual journey to shed and ward off shame. Oh, how this world and the enemy will use shame to strip us of who God intended us to be. Run, do not walk, to devour this book. Hold it tight; let Dr. Bengtson, and God, speak life into you through this encouraging book. I am praying for your healing and restoration!"

Rachel Joy Baribeau, author of *Relentless Joy*, former national sportscaster, and founder of #ImChangingtheNarrative

"We all have them—scars, that is—but few of us realize that these scars might just represent our finest hour. Dr. Michelle Bengtson teaches us to display our scars for God's glory rather than hide them, ignore them, or feel shame because of them. I read every word of *Sacred Scars* and felt hope return to my weary soul because I have scars too, and yet I haven't always known what to do with them. Now, because of Michelle's perspective, I will view my scars as the vehicle through which I am invited into his presence, where there is always fullness of joy."

Carol McLeod, speaker, bestselling author of *Rooms of a Mother's Heart* and *Meanwhile*, and host of the *Significant Women* podcast

"It's so easy to get stuck in the pain of our past . . . all the *would haves*, *could haves*, and *should haves* that bring guilt, shame, and/or regret. Dr. Michelle combines her contagious encouragement with years of professional experience as a neuropsychologist to help you move forward to see God's redemptive hand in your painful past. She hands you a dose of hope to see a bright future. If you are carrying a heavy past, unsure of what your next steps should be, or struggling to understand why things have happened the way they have, don't miss this book! And get one for your friend, too, because we all need to see our scars as something sacred."

Erica Wiggenhorn, national speaker with Aspire Women's Events and author of *An Unexpected Revival*

"We all have scars. Some are visible, but many are hidden beneath layers of emotional, relational, or even spiritual harm. The trials that cause these scars can lead us to wrestle with God and ask him hard questions, regardless of how strong our faith is. Using equal parts empathy, vulnerability, and intellect, board-certified clinical neuropsychologist Dr. Michelle Bengtson is the friend you want to help you navigate your pain and shame. And of course, her message is covered in her steadfast faith in Jesus. *Sacred Scars* is for anyone bearing scars—no matter how old—who is seeking purpose, understanding, and perspective in them. Using personal stories from both herself and others, Dr. Michelle comes alongside those who are suffering to offer empathy, encouragement, and the hope of Jesus. You are not alone."

Amy Connell, *Graced Health* podcast host and author of *Your Worthy Body* and *Your CORE Strength*

"With wisdom, love, and compassion, Dr. Michelle Bengtson encourages us to embrace God's unwavering love, which will empower us to rise above our pain and suffering and embrace blessings that emerge from our brokenness. God never forsakes us, especially during our most challenging times. You will find grace, peace, and promise through the intimate stories of those who have endured unimaginable suffering—emotionally, physically, and spiritually. This book is a compelling tribute to the human spirit and God's unfailing love."

Lee Ann Mancini, adjunct professor at South Florida Bible College & Theological Seminary, founder of the Raising Christian Kids nonprofit organization, and author and executive producer of the Sea Kids series

"Don't suffer alone, my friend. This book by Dr. Michelle Bengtson is the companion you need to heal your battle wounds and embrace your holy, sacred scars. Whether you've experienced an unexpected diagnosis, wounds at the hand of another, or consequences of your own mistakes, *Sacred Scars* offers real help and hope. This inspiring and easy-to-read resource reminds you that no pain is wasted in the hands of your loving Father. From her own sacred journey, Dr. Michelle shares practical ways to recognize 'the melody of love that God sings over us.' Through the pages you'll find courage amid the storm, determination to rely on Jesus when life doesn't make sense, and hope to face your redeemed future through the eyes of your heavenly Father, who makes all things new. One of my favorite quotes from this book: 'Some of our greatest growth opportunities come after the wrestle with pain and suffering.' May it be true for you as well."

Rhonda Stoppe, the No Regrets Woman, Christian speaker, bestselling author of *Moms Raising Sons to Be Men*, and host of the *Old Ladies Know Stuff* podcast

"I've been writing for a long time, but the hardest thing I've ever done was share my personal story and scars in my most recent book. Dr. Michelle Bengtson does just this in her beautiful book *Sacred Scars*. I appreciate and applaud her bravery, and I guarantee that you, like me, will be inspired, encouraged, and blessed by her story. We all have scars. They make us who we are, but not everyone does the work to learn from them and realize the power of sharing them. As Michelle prays, 'Father . . . help them to trust you in the waiting as you heal their wounds and bring beauty from their ashes in the form of sacred scars.' And as I like to say, 'God never wastes our pain.' I pray for you what this book echoes: May God bring purpose from your past into your future, and from this day on, may you realize how powerful your testimony is and how many lives can be changed by sharing it with others."

Greg Atkinson, author, speaker, founder of the First Impressions Conference and the Entrepreneurial Church Conference

"When I consider my physical body, the visible scars are obvious. It is my scarred emotional and spiritual state that remains hidden to the naked eye. The cavern of those sacred scars is dark, deep, and often disturbing. Posts about long nights of pain, agony, and anguish won't appear on my social media feed. I hide the hard and share the sensational. Who wants to hear about my suffering? Thankfully, in *Sacred Scars*, Dr. Michelle Bengtson does share her suffering with us. Writing a book about sacred scars means she has them. The truth within her words is palpable. Her honesty assures me that I can make it through my own journey. She writes, 'We may feel anonymous, unnamed, or unknown . . . pained, scarred, and discarded, and yet God calls us his own.' The juxtaposition of being scarred and being known as God's own can be a tough concept to grasp, but as Dr. Michelle promises in the beginning, '[our scars] *always* serve a purpose and impact us if we'll let them, because God never wastes our pain.'"

Janell Rardon, author, podcaster, board-certified life coach

"It is rare for me to find a book written by someone who not only writes experientially but also from a clinical as well as biblical perspective. Chapter 8 especially aligns with the core of my ministry, and Dr. Michelle has captured the heart of the matter in overcoming painful challenges: 'Perhaps overcoming isn't living a pain-free existence, but it's putting one foot in front of the other when everything within you begs you to quit.' If all a person derived from this book were to understand the truth of that one statement, it would be worth the read, but every page is filled with wisdom. I will be incorporating this into my recommended reading list for the clients I work with."

Dr. Mel Tavares, DMin in pastoral care and counseling, certified mental health coach, and life coach

"Dr. Michelle Bengtson's new book, *Sacred Scars*, captivated me. I found my personal life totally turned upside down in June 2023, when a stroke almost took me out of this world. Pain leaves profound footprints in our personal lives. How we respond to it can bring either healing or further trauma that can compound over time. Dr. Michelle walked with me personally, as well as in my profession, through the very dark days of my recovery. When I was given the honor of reading *Sacred Scars*, I again found a healing that enabled me to continue my path of recovery. I am personally and professionally indebted to Dr. Michelle Bengtson for her grace-filled, hope-filled, and hands-on care. As a certified professional life coach, I will continue to read and reread this book for myself and encourage all my clients to read it as an aid in their pursuit of physical, mental, emotional, relational, and spiritual healing of past pain."

Carolyn Freeman, counselor, certified professional life coach, and founder and president of Impact Coaching Ministries

"As a survivor of domestic abuse, I was terrified at the thought of God using my scars to help others. The scars were a constant reminder of the abuse I'd endured. I either tried to cover them and pretend they didn't exist, or I wore them as a badge of honor, like a child showing off their skinned knee. *Sacred Scars* is a book that would have helped me on my journey to healing. But it will take you on a journey to deeper healing to release the trauma and shame without spiritualizing your pain. God turns the ugliness of your pain into good, wasting nothing, when you face your pain with boldness and courage, which isn't easy. Michelle doesn't just use her story; she uses the stories of others who discovered God in their pain and now choose to use their pain to help others."

Karen DeArmond Gardner, author of *Hope for Healing from Domestic Abuse*, trauma advocate for women in or out of domestic abuse, and founder of Another One Free

"*Sacred Scars* is an essential and uncomplicated exploration of the suffering and resulting scars in our lives. Dr. Bengtson pairs biblical wisdom with real-life experience as she draws her readers always toward hope. 'God doesn't call all of us who have endured great pain and loss to lead Bible studies, write books, start ministries, or speak from stages,' writes Michelle. 'But he never wastes our pain, and he partners with those who are willing and surrendered to share out of the overflow of their heart after he has brought healing to them as well as sacred scars to honor the battle they've fought.' A compelling and meaningful reference."

Cindee Snider Re, author and cofounder of Chronic Joy

"Michelle Bengtson's *Sacred Scars* layers understanding and encouragement with biblical teaching on the aftermath of pain—whether that's emotional or physical. She provides sound counsel about how not to let a painful past dominate our present life or occlude our future. She tackles tough subjects such as woundedness and shame, providing direction on how to find a new identity that is stronger, more informed, and more compassionate toward ourselves and others. As someone who has experienced injustice, loss, and heartache, I found a friend in the pages of this book. I recommend it highly without reservation."

Janet Holm McHenry, national speaker and author of numerous books on prayer, including *The Complete Guide to the Prayers of Jesus*

"As someone who used to believe God could never use the painful parts of my story, I found *Sacred Scars* to be a healing balm that reassures us how dearly loved we are because our Savior bears scars, too, which highlight our redemption. Dr. Michelle Bengtson does a beautiful job covering us in truth and reminding us how our scars should not point toward shame but toward strength in Christ! Our past doesn't disqualify us. It demonstrates the power of a God who restores, mends, and makes all things new. This message is one all our hearts need."

Becky Beresford, speaker, coach, and author of *She Believed HE Could, So She Did*

SACRED
SCARS

Other Books by Dr. Michelle Bengtson

Hope Prevails:
Insights from a Doctor's Personal Journey through Depression

Breaking Anxiety's Grip:
How to Reclaim the Peace God Promises

Today Is Going to Be a Good Day:
90 Promises from God to Start Your Day Off Right

The Hem of His Garment:
Reaching Out to God When Pain Overwhelms

SACRED SCARS

Resting in God's Promise
That Your Past Is Not Wasted

DR. MICHELLE BENGTSON

Revell

a division of Baker Publishing Group
Grand Rapids, Michigan

Published by Revell Books
a division of Baker Publishing Group
Grand Rapids, Michigan
RevellBooks.com

Printed in the United States of America

Library of Congress Cataloging-in-Publication Data
Names: Bengtson, Michelle, author.
Title: Sacred scars : resting in God's promise that your past is not wasted / Dr. Michelle Bengtson.
Description: Grand Rapids, Michigan : Revell, a division of Baker Publishing Group, [2024] | Includes bibliographical references.
Identifiers: LCCN 2023048257 | ISBN 9780800742362 (paperback) | ISBN 9780800745806 (casebound) | ISBN 9781493445479 (ebook)
Subjects: LCSH: Pain—Religious aspects—Christianity. | Suffering—Religious aspects—Christianity. | Providence and government of God—Christianity.
Classification: LCC BV4909 .B469 2024 | DDC 248.8/6—dc23/eng/20231201
LC record available at https://lccn.loc.gov/2023048257

Cover design by Laura Powell

The author is represented by Illuminate Literary Agency, www.illuminateliterary.com.

Baker Publishing Group publications use paper produced from sustainable forestry practices and postconsumer waste whenever possible.

24 25 26 27 28 29 30   7 6 5 4 3 2 1

This book is dedicated to my mother:

You endured many physical, emotional, relational, and spiritual wounds in your short life, and yet your sacred scars gave me a legacy of faith, determination, grit, fortitude, endurance, and perseverance that have served me well. I pray my life and my pain-filled past glorify God as much as yours did. I look forward to a pain-free eternity together! All my love . . .

Contents

Introduction

Pain. There is pain all around us. If we aren't experiencing physical, emotional, relational, or spiritual pain now, either we recently have, we likely soon will, or we are walking alongside someone in the trenches who wonders if they will survive. For many, this world is a treacherous place, and pain and sorrow seem daily on the horizon. There is no escaping the pain of this life until God calls us home, but there is hope in the waiting. There are lessons to be gleaned from the wilderness. There are promises we've been given as a lifeline when no one else can offer assurances.

Friend, I don't know what variety of pain you're walking through or have recently survived, but I want you to know you're not alone and God doesn't waste our pain. Time and distance may make sharing over coffee together an impossibility, but you're in my thoughts, in my heart, and in my prayers as I type these words. I want you to know you *will* get through this, of that I'm certain. How can I be so certain, you ask? Have you not so far survived every single difficult circumstance in your life one hundred percent of the time? You have. You're here now. Those trials may not have turned out exactly as you'd hoped, and you may have made a few mistakes along the way. We're all flawed, and that's okay. You may have the bumps, bruises, and scars in the form of loss, grief, shame, guilt, or regret to show for the battles you fought, but that means you SURVIVED!

If we were sitting on my patio together, watching the cows graze next door, me with my coffee in hand and you with your beverage of choice, I'd hope that you would share about your battle wounds and scars. Each one tells an important story and helps create the narrative of who you are. And each one is sacred. God doesn't treat your scars lightly. Nor does he ignore their impact on your life. He doesn't just use your scars as a tool. God shapes your scars and shapes you in the process. You are braver, stronger, more tenacious, more resilient, and more beautiful for them.

> **God shapes your scars and shapes you in the process. You are braver, stronger, more tenacious, more resilient, and more beautiful for them.**

Your scars are valuable, as are the stories they tell. Your scars may not be physical scars that can be seen by the eye but may be emotional scars, relationship scars, grief-born scars, or even spiritual scars—scars that can be perceived and understood only through the wisdom and experience of a fellow sufferer. And some scars may be known only by God. Friend, I don't know the pain you've endured or the scars you now carry, but I have found that, much like soldiers on the front lines of war, we can endure much more when we know we aren't in the muck alone.

When we're in a painful battle, we wonder, *Will I make it through this? How will this change my life?* and *Is there purpose in my pain?* Loneliness often accompanies the crucible of pain, and we long to know we aren't alone in our suffering and that someone else understands. It's then that reading the stories of others who have walked similar paths has the potential to most encourage our hearts. And once we've come through the furnace of suffering, we can share our stories with others who feel the way we once did. Sometimes our stories encourage others to stay the course. Many times, stories inform and give hard-earned wisdom to someone just a few rungs down on the ladder of their own journey. Often, they inspire us to reach beyond what we thought we were capable of. Occasionally, they redirect the course of our future. But they *always* serve a purpose and impact us if we'll let them, because God never wastes our pain.

I pray that through the pages of this book, you will take my hand to hold and hear my heart: you are not alone in the battle. I hope each of the stories you read, and the sacred scars they represent, offer you strands of hope that you can weave into a lifeline when your own hope wanes. These are real people who have fought real battles and have the scars to prove it. Let their stories encourage you, inform you, teach you, motivate you, and comfort you. Just like in my other books, at the end of each chapter I've provided a recommended playlist of songs to encourage you on your healing journey. The entire playlist can be found at DrMichelleBengtson.com/Resources/Playlists. I've also given you "A Scarred Perspective," a biblical promise to hold on to until your wounds are fully healed and your sacred scars formed. Growth and healing often take place within community, and sometimes we don't see our potential or recognize God's hand at work in our lives until others bring it to our attention. At the end of the book, I've provided study questions that correspond to each chapter for your personal reflection and application or to use as a springboard for group study or book club discussion.

Once we've finished our coffee, and you've shared about your scars, and I've affirmed you with a few of my own, I would offer to pray for you. Not because there is anything special or powerful about my prayers but because all power exists from the One who answers. In lifting you to his ear and his heart, I leave you in the best hands possible, because even when our time together comes to an end, he will never leave you, and his healing continues!

> He heals the brokenhearted
> and binds up their wounds. (Ps. 147:3)

Father, I lift up the one holding this book in their hands, reading each page. They have sacred scars that only you may know. But the pages of their story, tear-stained as they may be, have woven a narrative that makes them beautifully and uniquely them. Would you encourage their heart to know that you hold not only their tears in your bottle but their scars in your heart as precious, sacred offerings on this screenplay of life for which you have cast them? Help them to see your hand in and through their sacred scars and to know you better for it. Extend your hand, steady their feet, and walk them through their pain and through the stories their scars tell, to come to the place where they know you never waste their pain. In Jesus's name, amen.

Friend, your pain, your wounds, and your scars are in good hands.

Admiring your scars from afar,
Dr. Michelle

⁘ Recommended Playlist ⁘

"Into the Sea (It's Gonna Be Ok)," Tasha Layton, © 2022 by BEC Recordings

"Don't Lose Heart," Steven Curtis Chapman, © 2022 by Provident Label Group, LLC

"You're Gonna Be Okay," Bethel Music, © 2021 by Bethel Music

"Make It Through," Leanna Crawford, © 2023 by Provident Label Group, LLC

"Take This," Out of the Dust, © 2019 by Out of the Dust

ONE

The Stories Our Scars Tell

> They triumphed over him
>   by the blood of the Lamb
>   and by the word of their testimony;
> they did not love their lives so much
>   as to shrink from death.
>
> Revelation 12:11

Several years ago, a television advertisement featured two old men in swimsuits at a public pool. Instead of getting after their exercise, they stood on the edge of the pool comparing scars in a humorous attempt to one-up each other by pointing out the physical reminders of accidents and surgical experiences. These were boast-worthy scars worn with pride.

Similarly, you might recall classmates who showed up to elementary school with a bright-white plaster cast on an arm or a leg. As traumatic as the precipitating event may have been, other classmates quickly surrounded the cast bearer, seeking the details and desiring a chance to add their initials, graffiti, and well-wishes to the cast with colorful felt-tip pens. Some of the cast wearers carried their own favorite-colored felt-tips! The pain and trauma were clearly diminished by the increased attention and social status the cast conferred. Those scars became social magnets.

One of our sons recently made a foray into the world of snowboarding. Thankfully, he donned a helmet for the endeavor (he basically had little choice or he knew one day his neuropsychologist mother would find out and give him what for!) before taking a tumble down a hill that left him with a gash, which has now turned into an endearing memorial scar. The events that precipitated that scar were rather humbling, so he has taken to regaling friends and family with ever-changing tales that grow more grandiose and outlandish with each passing year.

Recently, a young quarterback on a professional football team was asked at a postgame press conference how he handles the comments of those who question his abilities. His response was, "I carry my scars everywhere I go. I don't forget."[1] Very few of us forget the circumstances that precipitated our scars. He added that he's moved on and that he doesn't waste his energy worrying about someone else's opinion and prefers to focus on improving his performance.

On the Other Side

How is it that these artifacts that we universally associate with trauma, pain, and loss come to carry pride, social status, or motivation? Is it the passage of time? The approval of others? Some shift in perspective? What kind of commentary would we hear from these individuals if we could rewind the clock to the moment of the trauma or error? Illness or disease, accident, public humiliation . . . I don't think any of us would speak with confidence or humor in those moments. These are the events that take time to heal from. At the time, those in the examples above would have had a vastly different affect, certainly lacking the humor, social engagement, and confident calmness that mark their anecdotes. These events likely initially elicited frustration, confusion, anger, embarrassment, despair, fear, shock, or grief. In a moment, or in time, pain would come   physical, emotional, social, or spiritual pain, or the pain of guilt, shame, regret, or loss.

Yet these examples are of individuals who have clearly survived the event. They are, to some degree, on the other side, with sacred scars to show for it. Their journeys and the personal changes wrought are interesting to us. Why? Because we know that their journeys were difficult and required the personal courage of facing adversity and persevering. To some degree, in our own pain, we want the encouragement that if they made it through, maybe we can too.

It is archetypal to view an individual who has persevered as a hero, a survivor, or an overcomer. We view them as strong, confident, and capable, thinking, *If they could handle* that, *is there anything they can't handle? Or I wish I had the courage, confidence, compassion, or understanding they display. Or If only I could gain the capability, outcome, or result they've achieved!* Hollywood knows this. It's the basis for most movies—a sympathetic hero facing an unexpected and undeserved but daunting challenge. Inevitably, we are on the edge of our seats, pulling for the good guy to triumph. It's also something most marketers know. Think about the numerous advertisements where some beautiful actor describes massive weight loss or the development of large and obvious muscles. They generally claim that "with product X and a few short weeks, you can look like this," with the implicit understanding that losing the flab or developing cinema-worthy abs will deliver the confidence we lack or the status we crave. These pitches are usually delivered with a focus on the bright, shiny product and not the sweat, pain, and suffering that go with it to achieve the results portrayed.

We see ourselves in those stories, in those advertisements, and even in the funny commercials, like the one with the two old men. In some way they describe us because even if the precipitating circumstances are different, pain is universal. We know that life is challenging. It comes with suffering and adversity, and we can see them displayed in the stories we hear and in the lives of those around us. We like to hope that we would respond positively in similar circumstances, but we wonder. We wonder if we have the right stuff to get through it, even if we can't describe "the right stuff" or explain what "get through it" means. So we look for heroes, people who have been there, who have survived or come out the other side. Seeing the triumph of others, even in fictional accounts, assures us that it can be done. It gives us narratives in which we can vicariously see ourselves winning or overcoming.

Changed Somehow

But what of the suffering or sweat or work that comes with the stories those scars tell? We know it isn't all glory and honor. We don't cheer for the person lying on the couch, eating chocolate, and binge-watching Netflix. We cheer for Rocky—the guy who is struggling, who's trying, who's persevering despite the pain. Even in the losing, we see the value of the effort, of the valiance, of the wholehearted engagement. But we have an approach-avoidance perspective to the sufferings and scars of life. We admire those who come through, but we don't want to personally suffer the circumstances. We admire the outcomes—the understanding, courage, conviction, or confidence—but we'd much rather take a pill to achieve them instead of putting in hard, focused, continuing work, or worse, personal suffering and pain.

In hearing these stories, we know that the people involved were changed somehow. They have scars to show a change— physical, emotional, mental, relational, spiritual, or otherwise. We can see it in their words, actions, or attitudes—a fear-lessness toward new situations, or a sensitivity to others, or wisdom, or appropriate caution replacing recklessness. Even without knowing a person deeply, it's still possible to see changes in their perspectives, priorities, or passions after they come out of a traumatic or aversive event. We can tell that they think differently about themselves, others, or the world around them.

We like to provide attribution to these changes. It's human to tag victory over a tragedy or circumstance as "triumph of the human spirit," or as a protagonist "finding their place in life" or "coming to terms with reality." It feels good to put a frame around something that is discomforting, that is maybe a little scary or dangerous to us, and that we don't fully understand. Is this really just an abstract projection, though? Is it believing in Hollywood or wanting to find *something* redeeming or virtuous in suffering? It lets us compartmentalize a fearful thing, but is it honest? Are we just voyeurs arm-chairing another's tragedy and imputing glorious motives to make ourselves feel better about the fates of life? Do we think that if we can describe them, then they won't be so scary, and maybe, just maybe, we will be less likely to fall under their sway?

Better, I think, to skip the attribution and to leave the arm-chair vacant. Better to ask the person in the arena. It is his story and his to feel the fear, loss, shame, guilt, or even victory. It is hers to bear the scars and to live the scarred life with sacred rev-erence. It is his to reap the benefits and blessings of the courage or compassion or conviction that may come from the suffering and scars, and hers to describe the rhythm and cadence of her daily walk during and after the fact.

We know that pain, suffering, and hardship fall into everyone's lives, whether we bring them upon ourselves or not. These experiences, physical, emotional, relational, or spiritual, often slash our esteem and confidence, kick at our resolve, and damage our own sense of identity and value. Painful trials often ignite or reignite regret, shame, fear, guilt, condemnation, or a sense of loss and lead to scarring, permanent marks of imperfection— either physical external scars or hidden internal scars known only to us and God. We perceive these scars as ugly, as marring something that once had value and displayed beauty but no longer does, like a cracked vase, a broken frame, or a scratched tabletop. We come to believe that the wounds and brokenness of our dirty, messy lives, and their resulting scars, disqualify us from living a full and complete life. That they leave us marred and ugly, beauty-less and valueless in the sight of others and of God, like a chipped plate no longer safe to eat from.

As a board-certified clinical neuropsychologist, I have been given the honor and privilege of walking with my patients through their pain, hearing their most intimate stories—some they've never shared with anyone else—and witnessing their sacred scars. I've heard the stories of many people who confessed to believing that their past pain, mistakes, sins, and wounds, and the resulting emotional, physical, relational, or spiritual scars, made them less lovable, less qualified, or less valued in their own estimation or in the sight of others and of God.

A Platform of Preparation

Although we fear the events that scar us and we view scars negatively, they are often the platform of preparation God uses to draw us to himself, to show us who we really are, to highlight new facets of his character for us to experience, and to powerfully demonstrate the preciousness with which he holds us—a preciousness that goes beyond human understanding. Through these transformations God trains us for the plans and purposes he defined for us before we were born, plans and purposes to know and live this incredible worth with which he esteems us and to share it unashamedly and compassionately with other wounded and broken people.

Have you grown weary? Have you played by the rules, taken the high road, sacrificed, prayed, believed, hoped, and worked but still feel like resolution eludes you? Maybe you know joy comes in the morning, but your night has grown dark and long, and it hasn't felt like morning in a long time. I don't know why your season has prevailed so long, but I do know this: *there is purpose in our pain.* I know of no one I deeply admire or respect who hasn't walked through dark and difficult days. Those I know who are called upon to do great things and fulfill great destiny walk through fire and flood and famine first. Take heart. You are not alone!

Let this trial have its perfect work in you as the testing of your faith produces endurance and the heat and pressure form your lump-of-coal character into a diamond of clarity and brilliance and beauty. I know you're tired. I know you are low on strength and perhaps lower on morale, but don't give up. This is the prayer of my heart for you, so let me pray for you now:

> *God, strengthen this weary soul. Show them just a glimpse of heaven's perspective, like when you looked down upon your servant Job. Bear them up. Cause them to feel your presence and allow your joy to become their strength. Breathe on them and help them to trust not only your sovereignty but also your affection and concern and care. Let them hear your voice, whether in the pit or prison or palace, and know that you are God Almighty, their glory and the lifter of their head. In Jesus's name, amen.*

Don't allow this trial to push you past your hope or cause you to stop pursuing your dreams. Lean into it. Push with the pain, like a woman in labor. Use it to birth your future. See the joy set before you and take courage to stand another day.

My story is one that is filled with hurt, mistakes, regrets, broken pieces, ugly truths, and shards of pain I would prefer to keep locked in a box. And yet each morning God gives me breath and reminds me that my story is also filled with grace that pulled me out of the pit of despair, unexpected healing and recovery, peace that made no sense, a declaration of value and identity, and a deeper relationship with my heavenly Father. This is the Father who sustains me and gives me the strength to persevere when the tenuous and weaker side of me is tempted to wave the white flag of surrender and give up.

My friend, God doesn't play favorites. He loves each one of his children completely, unconditionally, and intimately. When Christ died on the cross, he did so for each one of us. What God has done to bring beauty from the ashes of my pain, and the pain of others who share their stories in the following pages, he longs to do for you as well.

Through the stories of others, ancient and contemporary, we will look at how pain and suffering inflict wounds, then become scars, but then reveal a treasure of transformation, redemption, and purpose. Many have been scarred by life's thorny path and now have an identifiable "mark" to show how God comforted them and brought them to a level place where the beauty of their scars is now greater than their pain. In the coming pages you will read stories of persevering and overcoming and of finding encouragement in community, but mostly of the faithfulness and presence of a personal God, of his revelation to each storyteller of true beauty, value, and identity made visible through their sacred scars.

The pain points of today, the battle wounds you continue to fight—those that remain tender to the touch if not a bit bruised in your heart—will heal in time. The scars of your previous life scuffles no longer represent open wounds but symbolize a road map of the healing God has provided, even if it's still unfinished, and testify to his unchanging character. It is my hope that as you learn to honor your scars as sacred to God, you will begin to appreciate just how far you've come so that on the painful days your heart will be encouraged to stay the course. My prayer is that you will come to know how beautiful God thinks you are and that you will give him your guilt, shame, and regret over the things that caused you pain. I pray that you would see the incredible value he places on you and recognize the identity in him that he offers, and that you would allow him to redeem your suffering as he heals your wounds and seals your sacred scars. Your pain and your scars are precious to God as an offering of your life for him to mold and shape in the process. Sometimes seeing the purpose in the pain of others helps us identify God's redemption in our own stories. I pray that you will be blessed by the stories of others' sacred scars in the coming pages.

Many have been scarred by life's thorny path and now have an identifiable "mark" to show how God comforted them and brought them to a level place where the beauty of their scars is now greater than their pain.

A Scarred Perspective

This High Priest of ours understands our weaknesses, for he faced all of the same testings we do, yet he did not sin. (Heb. 4:15 NLT)

My Prayer for You

Father, this precious child of yours has gone through the crucible of pain. Help them to trust you in the waiting as you heal their wounds and bring beauty from their ashes in the form of sacred scars. Assure them that you never waste their pain and you bring purpose from their past into their future. We look to you not just for healing but also for redemption of that which was lost, stolen, or broken. In Jesus's name, amen.

Recommended Playlist

"Scars," I AM THEY, © 2018 by Provident Label Group, LLC

"Hard Times Prelude," Jason Gray, © 2020 by Centricity Music

"Don't You Dare," Ginny Owens, © 2021 by Chick Power Music

"God Is in This Story," Katy Nichole and Big Daddy Weave, © 2023 by Centricity Music

"Even When You're Broken," Julie Yardley, © 2013 by Skylight Productions

TWO

Scars Signify a Battle

You come against me with sword and spear and javelin, but I come against you in the name of the LORD Almighty, the God of the armies of Israel, whom you have defied.

1 Samuel 17:45

When you look back over the landscape of your life, are there deep wounds you keep hidden from the rest of the world? What do you cover up so others won't see? What negative experiences have you gone through or mistakes have you made that you believe disqualify you from something greater in your future because you don't have things "all together"? Are there physical, emotional, relational, or spiritual hurts, wounds, pains, disgraces, or traumas that have significantly and negatively impacted the lens through which you view your life?

Just weeks after I turned in the manuscript for my book *Breaking Anxiety's Grip*, my husband and I were driving to an appointment when my cell phone rang. On the other end was my doctor, who had run some tests only days before. Upon answering, I heard the words no one expects nor wants to hear: "I hate to have to tell you this, Dr. Bengtson, but you have cancer."

I have no idea what she said next. I was already reacting. *What? That can't be—I'm healthy, I exercise daily, I eat well (as long as you consider an occasional piece of chocolate at least good for the soul, if not good for the body). They must have the wrong patient.*

"Dr. Bengtson, are you there?"

"What? I mean yes. Sorry, I was just processing what you said."

"I understand. We need to schedule you for surgery right away. Would you like to schedule that now?"

I'm sure what proceeded to pour from my lips sounded more like a stutter or stammer than intelligible words. "Um, no. I, um, will have to get back to you on that. We're just about to step into an appointment for my husband. I'll have to look at my calendar and get back to you."

I didn't hear her final words. I sat staring straight ahead out the windshield as the same phrase played repeatedly in my mind, just like when the needle gets stuck on an old vinyl record and keeps playing the same several notes. "I've got cancer. I've got c-a-n-c-e-r. Oh my word . . . how can this be? I've got cancer."

My husband's voice broke my free fall into the dark abyss in my mind. "Honey? Is everything all right?"

"No . . . the doctor said I have cancer."

Moments later, we sat waiting at his appointment. As the shock began to wear off, fear threatened to assault. I knew in that moment that I had a choice to make: either I could acquiesce to the enemy's temptation for me to fear, for my future and for my family, *or* I could trust that this diagnosis hadn't taken God by surprise and he would care for me regardless of what my future held.

I'll never forget the shock and horror I felt when weeks later, after the dreaded surgery, I stared at my mirrored reflection in disgust when the surgical bandages were removed and I saw my scarred flesh. I didn't even notice my face or my neatly coiffed hair. All I could see was the wound that remained as a testament of the cancer that had invaded my body. The scarlet zigzag was raised, tender, and unsightly. Nothing would hide cancer's indelible mark.

The pain that ensued was a hurtful, nagging reminder of the part of my history I would have preferred to forget. Yet even as the pain subsided, the scar served as a virtual billboard that flashed, "Here . . . it was here. And because of it, you are forever changed."

I hated that scar and all it represented. Even as others prayed for my complete healing, the enemy was quick to whisper, *If God really loved you, this never would have happened. Now you are broken and flawed. Your imperfection is forever on display.*

Over the following days, weeks, months, and year, I wrestled with God. I knew God hadn't inflicted this disease on me. He says in his Word that it is his desire that we prosper and be in health, even as our soul prospers (see 3 John 1:2). I clung to the promise that what the enemy intended for evil in my life, God would use for good (see Gen. 50:20). I desired to learn what God had for me in this and to know that the pain of the experience would not be wasted. But as I stared at my scar in the mirror, I wondered out loud, "How could something so ugly ever become something good?"

We rarely recognize the purpose of pain and the resulting scars at the time. In the waiting, in the praying, in the trusting, God is working his will and his way to help us become a brighter reflection of him. His promises give us countless reasons to hope. Throughout my husband's and my health-related battles, I clung to Psalm 27:13: "I remain confident of this: I will see the goodness of the LORD in the land of the living." When facing pain and adversity, it helps to speak God's promises instead of reciting the problem. Not only does God own the cattle on a thousand hills, but he also owns all the hills! He is a good God, his plans for us are good, and he longs to be our Provider. But growth is a process, one that we can't rush, especially when we want God's outcome.

What Is a Scar?

When the body is wounded, it goes into battle mode and immediately begins a complex process of healing. This healing process results in the formation of a scar. Scars are a natural part of the healing process and are formed when the body creates new tissue to repair damaged skin. Physical scars are made when the body's natural maintenance processes are disrupted, such as by a deep cut, burn, surgery, or other injury that damages the skin's surface.

The formation of a scar begins with the inflammatory response, which is the body's way of protecting itself from infection. When the skin is cut, blood vessels are damaged, causing bleeding and inflammation. The body responds by sending white blood cells to the site of the injury to fight off any potential infection. Next, the body begins the process of filling in the wound with new tissue, which is made up of new blood vessels, collagen, and other types of cells. This network of cells is stronger and more durable than the original skin, but it doesn't have the same texture or color as the surrounding skin. As the wound continues to heal, the body produces more collagen, a protein that helps strengthen the new tissue. The collagen fibers are similar to the skin's natural tissue but lack certain details, such as hair follicles and sweat glands, making scars different from healthy skin. The amount and distribution of collagen fibers determine the type of scar that forms, which can range from barely noticeable to raised, thick, or discolored. Over time, scars may begin to fade or flatten and become less noticeable as the body continues to produce collagen and remodel the tissue, but they typically remain visible as a permanent reminder of the injury. Regardless of their appearance, scars are the evidence of being made new but only occur *after* healing has taken place.

Scars Take Time

When my husband and I were newlyweds, I longed for a garden. But we also anticipated moving into a new home. Unsure of when this would happen, we constructed a mobile garden on casters so that when we moved, it could move with us. We built the frame, filled it with soil, and planted the seeds. Over the next few days, I diligently watered, waited, and watched for new growth. After several days, I impatiently wondered where my garden was because all I could see was dirt. In retrospect, there was plenty happening there, but it was all slow and underground—I just couldn't see it.

We rarely recognize the value of the pain and scars at the time. In the waiting, in the praying, in the trusting, God is invisibly working. Like with my invisible garden, the change is there, but it's often slow and underground. Growth is a process, and no amount of wanting or willing things to change is going to rush what's necessary. The same is true of our pain. When pain hits, we desperately want healing, and we want it yesterday. But it takes time for healing to occur, and we can either begrudge the pain or embrace the process. We can either grow bitter and resentful or look to God with expectancy for who he is and what he is doing.

Our scars are the tapestry of the lessons we've learned through pain.

My friend, *our scars are not a bad thing*! Our scars are the tapestry of the lessons we've learned through pain, whether those scars are the result of physical, emotional, relational, or spiritual pain. Scars signify a battle has occurred. As he does his healing work in our lives, Jesus is glorified in and through our scars since we reflect more of him because of our suffering. The very scars that I viewed as unsightly are the ones that others connect with in their own pain, because they are real, raw, and relatable. My surgical scars have begun to fade over time, but the lessons have not. And if you can hold on to the lessons and stories your sacred scars tell, you will see God's redemptive hand in them.

Living in a Fallen World

Because we live in a fallen, evil world, pain and adversity are inevitable, but how we respond to such experiences is our choice and will significantly impact how we live in the future. Will we allow our scars to limit us, or will we use them to inform who we are and how we interact with others? As I said in my book *The Hem of His Garment*, "If you aren't going through a painful time right now, you either just came out of one or are preparing to enter one."[1] In that book, we looked at the inevitability of experiencing the different types of pain at some point during our lifetime. For some, pain is physical, while for others, it is emotional, and still others experience relational or spiritual pain. Regardless of the shape, form, or presentation of our pain, none of us can escape it in this life. A great deal of the suffering experienced because of pain is the result of a simultaneous desire for healing and the dread that pain will never cease. I believe God never intended for us to know pain, suffering, or adversity—he intended for us to know him. But the fall of creation ushered in every type of pain imaginable, and the enemy uses that to his advantage, knowing that pain has consequences: "Pain colors our perspective, robs us of the best parts of us, and challenges us to just barely cling to the hem of Jesus's garment."[2]

Pain is like the dirty road we tread in sandaled feet as we move across the landscape of our lives. We all have something that we keep hidden in the deep recesses of our hearts, hoping no one will find it. Sins we've committed, mistakes we've made, poor decisions, physical or emotional struggles, or experiences that have in some way pained us and left a scar on our bodies, in our minds, or in our hearts. Jesus warned us that we would all experience times of pain, trouble, or suffering.

> I have told you these things, so that in Me you may have [perfect] peace. In the world you have tribulation *and* distress *and* suffering, but be courageous [be confident, be undaunted, be filled with joy]; I have overcome the world. [My conquest is accomplished, My victory abiding.] (John 16:33 AMP, italics in the original)

Notice that his offer of peace is not isolated from our times of pain. We can have peace while experiencing pain because he has already won our ultimate victory for us. That victory is represented in the scars he bore as well as those we eventually bear.

Decades ago, I enjoyed doing counted cross-stitch in my spare time. Our home was filled with pictures, towels, boxes, Christmas stockings, and jewelry made from my carefully stitched canvases. During the process of creating, I tended to focus on the ugliness of the backside where all my colored threads started, stopped, intertwined, and knotted together. But once the project was completed and it could be seen as the work of art it was, the back no longer begged for my attention because the completed work was all that mattered. To a large degree, the same is true of our lives. During our difficult trials, we tend to focus on the pain and our desire for healing. But ultimately, our scars represent the beautiful, merciful healing of a good God who redeems and makes all things new in his own way and in his perfect time. While we tend to see the ugly, knotted mass of our pain and suffering, and the physical, emotional, relational, or spiritual fallout, Jesus sees the beautiful tapestry created by the highs and the lows, the good and the bad, and the pain and the scars of our lives.

I am indebted to God because he provided not just his holy Word for us to learn about him and his ways but also the stories of biblical greats who went before us, whose lives were messy, dirty, broken, and often tumultuous. Each of their stories attests to the fact that God used broken, messed-up people with painful pasts to accomplish some of his greatest work, and in the process often provided healing for the individuals involved. Those stories and those works also include us. The accounts of not just their humanness but most certainly their struggles, mistakes, and triumphs encourage my heart. Most of what you and I will endure in our lives will not compare to the beatings, martyrdom, and imprisonment of some of God's greatest servants. That in no way takes away from our pain and suffering, but it gives us hope that if they could survive and thrive, we can too. While our pain is great, his purposes are greater. The lessons learned, the empathy and compassion gained, the testimonies that follow are all part of God's great redemptive plan. He wastes nothing, my friend. Not even our pain.

A Giant in the Land

Scripture provides an account of a shepherd boy who didn't let the taunts and jeers of his older siblings diminish his courage and bravery to face the giant in the land. While we don't know many specifics about David's relationship with all his siblings, 1 Samuel 17:28 reveals the disdain David's oldest brother had toward David. We might surmise that David was picked on, demeaned, and disparaged by his other siblings. That kind of treatment often results in emotional and relational pain and can leave scars that impact our self-worth, confidence, and fortitude later in life. We don't know what wounds David endured as a shepherd protecting his family's flocks, but we know that he killed both lions and bears (see 1 Sam. 17:36). It's not a reach to think he dealt with fear in the moment, both fear for his life and fear about his adequacy for the task as the youngest and maligned son. Yet in the story of Goliath, we see David deflecting the barbs of his older brother, confidently approaching the king, choosing his own plan of battle, and fearlessly triumphing over the giant. Whatever wounds he'd endured had scarred over, and from them he developed great confidence in his skills and in the God whom he had become close to through the lonely days in the pasture. His scars reflected the preparation God provided him long before he would ever need his skills as a shepherd to fight for his family, his people, and his land against an imposing giant. Let his story be a reminder that our painful battles are the Lord's and we must place our faith wholeheartedly in God as our Preparer, Provider, Protector, and Victor.

Surviving the Battle

Scars signify that we've endured a battle and survived. From Scripture, we know the source of our battles: "For our struggle is not against flesh and blood, but against the rulers, against the authorities, against the powers of this dark world and against the spiritual forces of evil in the heavenly realms" (Eph. 6:12). The enemy of our soul is the source of pain, adversity, temptation, deception, and shame. God never created us to live a life of sin, pain, or adversity, but he will see us through it, teach us from it, and bring good out of it.

The enemy attempts to silence us because he knows the great impact of our testimonies. "They triumphed over him by the blood of the Lamb and by the word of their testimony" (Rev. 12:11). While not all our stories have happy endings, we do serve a God who can bring beauty from the ashes of our pain and work all our life experiences for our good and for his glory in and through our sacred scars (see Rom. 8:28).

John 10:10 reminds us that "the thief comes only to steal and kill and destroy; I have come that they may have life, and have it to the full." The enemy of our soul desires to steal our calling, kill our dreams, and destroy our destiny. Particularly with respect to Christ followers, the enemy works overtime trying to convince us that our sins, mistakes, and imperfect experiences should be hidden rather than used for good as part of God's great plan of redemption in and for our lives. I've counseled thousands who believed that arrest, infidelity, domestic violence, mental illness, bankruptcy, or some other blight in their past disqualified them from any good in their life, much less God's service, when the truth is that "in *all* things God works for the good of those who love him, who have been called according to his purpose" (Rom. 8:28, emphasis added).

> **God never created us to live a life of sin, pain, or adversity, but he will see us through it, teach us from it, and bring good out of it.**

My husband and I never wanted our health issues to be our primary focus. They are simply part of life's distractions. I want my focus to be on God and all he has done, is doing, will do, and wants me to do as we await complete and permanent healing, whether in this life or in the next. I live from the perspective that every setback is a setup for God to show off and do what only God can do. Some days the tsunami of pain threatens to pull me under, but my heart's desire is to be set on God, to glean whatever he most desires for me to learn in the process. Yet I strive for transparency in sharing the pain and the victories because I want others to know they aren't alone in the battle. My scars reflect the platform of my faith through which I face trials. The Lord encourages my heart through the comments of others that my faith helps them keep theirs amid their suffering, that my commitment to see things through God's perspective gives them hope in their own struggles, that my desire for God to be glorified in and through my pain challenges them to serve him with purpose.

In *The Phantom of the Opera*, the main character is deeply scarred and wears a mask to hide his disfigurement, metaphorically keeping others from seeing his true self. Throughout the play, we see the effects of his withdrawal and isolation on his life and the desperate risks he takes to find companionship. I wonder, how often do we hide behind a beautiful mask or a social media filter to cover our scars, our wounds, and the blemishes on the tapestry of our lives? How often do we carry the weight of inferiority because of our past pain and brokenness? How often do we judge ourselves unworthy of life's best because imperfection is reflected to us in the mirror? We may not recognize it, but I suspect most of us have wrestled with the impact and meaning the scars of our past life experiences have imposed on our present and even on our future. Scars signify a battle. To God, your sacred scars are beautiful and have significant purpose.

As you think back on your life, has anything happened to you that you would be embarrassed for others to know about? Have you made mistakes that you now regret and wish you could magically undo? Have you made decisions that negatively impacted the trajectory of your life? Have things been done to you that you've kept locked up in the secret recesses of your heart? Are there things that you believe you could never share with another individual because they are too scandalous or too embarrassing to admit? Those are the very things we often think disqualify us from being used by God. We mistakenly believe that God can only use perfect people. But, my friend, that's not true. God only uses imperfect people because, aside from his Son, Jesus, those are the only kind that exist! You can't mess up God's plan for you—you're just not that powerful.

A Scarred Perspective

He heals the brokenhearted
and binds up their wounds. (Ps. 147:3)

My Prayer for You

*Father, Jesus told us we would experience trials or battles
in this life. Let this dear one embrace the fact that their
scars signify they have endured a battle. Help them see
their battle scars as a beautiful reminder that you brought
them through to the other side. Their scars do not need
to be hidden but celebrated for how far they have come.
In Jesus's name, amen.*

Recommended Playlist

"Pieces," Meredith Andrews, © 2012 by Word
    Entertainment

"My Arms," Ledger, © 2020 by Atlantic Recording

"Start Over," Hope Darst, © 2020 by Hope Darst

"Before the Morning," Josh Wilson, © 2023 by Josh
    Wilson

"Even in the Heartache," Jonathan Jackson, © 2018 by
    Jonathan Jackson

THREE

Shame OFF You—
You Are Not Your Past

Guard my life and rescue me;
  do not let me be put to shame,
  for I take refuge in you.

Psalm 25:20

Ever since the garden of Eden, Satan has used shame to demean us and separate us from God. God knew Adam and Eve's condition; he created them and let them wander naked through the garden and rule over every living thing. After each thing God created, he declared it good, but after his most epic creation of humanity, he declared it not just good but *very* good (see Gen. 1:4–31).

The enemy never plays fair, and he always has our destruction as his goal. He tempted Eve (and by extension, Adam) to eat the fruit of the forbidden tree, and yet when they did, he rejoiced then shamed them. After they ate from the tree of the knowledge of good and evil and God called out to Adam, as he had done every day previously when he walked and talked with Adam and Eve in the garden, Adam's response was different. "He answered, 'I heard you in the garden, and I was afraid because I was naked; so I hid'" (Gen. 3:10). Adam had never hidden before; for that matter, he had never had a reason to fear before. Shame caused him to fear God and hide. There was no need to hide their nakedness from God—God had created them naked. But their sin changed their perception of their condition, and they feared God's response. Their sin led to shame and their shame led to fear. But God's perspective of us as his beloved children who are helpless to manage life on our own does not change.

As God loved and provided for Adam and Eve unchangingly, even after their sin, so he loves and provides for us. I learned about shame as a little girl when I was figuring out what was expected of me, how to function as part of a family unit, and the nuances of the English language.

The summer heat wafted in through the screen, the sliding glass door open ostensibly to let the breeze in and the heat out. The heat was so oppressive that I remember wondering as a young, elementary-school-aged child just how far the sweat droplets would travel down my back before getting stuck and lodging there. Dinner was grilled hot dogs (so the indoor oven didn't need to be used), iceberg-lettuce salad with a bit of shredded cheddar cheese and chopped hard-boiled egg thrown on top, and cucumbers soaked in vinegar, with sliced watermelon wedges for dessert . . . keeping things as cool as possible.

"Michelle, do you want to help Dad mow the lawn after dinner?" my mother asked.

I had visions of retreating to the cool cement floor in the basement to escape the summer cauldron and lying there until fall. "Not really," I replied with a child's casual honesty.

Riding in my father's lap on the lawn mower was fairly routine for me. At eight years old, I was not yet given independent access to the mower, but he allowed me to occasionally steer, with his hands at the ready. I didn't usually mind "helping" my dad, or at least keeping him company mowing the lawn; it was just what I did. But on this particular day, the early evening heat was oppressive with no shade in the yard, and from my juvenile understanding, my mother was offering me a choice. Did I want to help him? If offered the choice, I didn't really want to. If I was expected to, I would. And I would do it without complaining. But if it was expected, then why did she ask me about my desire?

"Shame on you!" was her reply.

Oh, the many times I heard that phrase throughout my life . . . either applied to me or someone around me. And each time it was spoken, I did feel shame, and part of my personality shrunk under the criticism. I felt inadequate. I felt like a rebellious adolescent rather than the rule follower I was. Over time, I began to wear that shame. That shame altered my perception of myself and how I understood God and his view of me. It set up a very defeating dynamic that caused me to think I had to earn God's love and acceptance, a common conviction but possibly one of the most misguided and harmful beliefs I ever held.

I lived much of my life under the cloak of shame. I was ashamed of the physical deformity that made me different from my peers, so I continuously tried to cover it up and make excuses for my noticeable limp. I was ashamed to be a fatherless teenager after my father died unexpectedly early from a massive heart attack. I was ashamed of my mother, who was depressed and withdrawn throughout my childhood and could come across as rather abrupt. I was ashamed of my body's rejection of the baby in my womb when I miscarried. I was ashamed when I didn't live up to the expectations I had set for myself (which, of course, amounted to perfection), much less those that others set. The shame I carried in so many facets of my life degraded my esteem, caused me to seek the approval of others, and always left me feeling like a failure and a disgrace to God. In shame, I retreated, hid, and pretended I was someone other than myself, and I carried that with me into adulthood.

Where Shame Leads

Like captives in isolated dungeons, we struggle in silence and increasing loneliness with shame and discouragement and with significance and identity. In our isolation, we become more vulnerable to attacks from our spiritual enemy. Friend, you are not alone, even when shame makes you believe you are, or that you want to be. If you are experiencing shame, be assured that message doesn't come from your heavenly Father but from the enemy of your soul, who hates you and is intent on destroying you.

Shame is described as "a feeling of embarrassment or humiliation that arises from the perception of having done something dishonorable, immoral, or improper."[1] Shame leaves us feeling unacceptable, unable, unworthy, unlovely, and even unlovable. It acts as an inner critic proclaiming our lack of worth or value because of what we've done or what has been done to us. It's in those times that we must know, understand, and accept God's truth about who we are, how he made us, and how extremely he loves us, to combat the darkness that settles deep within and clouds our hearts.

Shame is the precipitant of fear, and hiding and isolation are the consequences. Along with shame often come the ugly stepsiblings of guilt and regret. If gone unchecked, shame, guilt, and regret so color our perspective of ourselves that we begin to believe we have no worth, purpose, or direction out of the pain of our past, which translates into adopting the false identity that "I am a mistake" rather than "I made a mistake." God wants us to bring to him our guilt, shame, and regret since Christ, who loves us, has already paid the price for these burdens. We are image bearers of God and carry an identity rooted in who he is. "So God created man in his own image, in the image of God he created him; male and female he created them" (Gen. 1:27 ESV). Shame isolates (exactly what the enemy wants—to keep us far from God, who will remind us of his truth), whereas God welcomes us into holiness because Jesus has washed away our shameful past. "May God himself, the God of peace, sanctify you through and through. May your whole spirit, soul and body be kept blameless at the coming of our Lord Jesus Christ. The one who calls you is faithful, and he will do it" (1 Thess. 5:23–24). In this we lose the fear and isolation and are welcomed with grace and freedom into fellowship with God.

Sometimes it's difficult to recognize shame. The following are just some of the ways it presents. Shame looks like:

- sensitivity to the opinions of others
- allowing others to take advantage of you
- living with the belief that you are forever rejected and inadequate
- losing your identity to your sin, mistakes, mistreatment, or pain
- fearing criticism or failure
- feeling unworthy of someone else's company
- shutting people out
- avoiding being the center of attention

Shame causes us to hide—from others and from God. It makes us isolate and become defensive about those things we desire to keep hidden. Shame masks our identity, making it difficult (if not impossible) to recognize or agree with who God says we are.

Shame, guilt, and regret keep us tied up in the mistakes or happenings of the past, when God desires for us to walk forward into our future in his mercy and grace. "Therefore there is now no condemnation [no guilty verdict, no punishment] for those who are in Christ Jesus [who believe in Him as personal Lord and Savior]" (Rom. 8:1 AMP). In God's eyes, our past mistakes don't dictate our future because he instilled that in us before we were born. Each day is a new day to lean into God's mercy, grace, forgiveness, and freedom.

Shifted Identity

The enemy knows that if he can shift our perspective regarding our identity, we will live contrary to our identity in Christ, which offers forgiveness, healing, redemption, renewal, and the mind of Christ by the power of the Holy Spirit. That's why he works so hard to keep us wrapped up in our shameful past, all while God is beckoning us to bring to him our broken pieces, past mistakes, and shattered dreams to create something eternally more beautiful. You are not your past. While the pain of your past may inform you, it isn't and doesn't determine your identity . . . God does.

> **You are not your past. While the pain of your past may inform you, it isn't and doesn't determine your identity . . . God does.**

My friend Leeann went through a painful marriage that impacted how she perceived herself and colored her identity. Gradually, as she learned to give God her pain and make him primary in her life, God healed her heart and began using her to help facilitate healing in others. To help others see themselves as God sees them and work toward healthier marriages. Leeann shares:

I was married almost twenty years the first time. Nobody expects to have to say, "the first time." I struggled through this marriage, making my husband an idol and looking to please him over anything else. I lived for his approval and when he rejected me in favor of intimacy with others, I became suicidal and depressed. We were five years in and I was pregnant before I knew about my husband's unfaithfulness. This attacked the foundation of our marriage and the core of my identity. The divorce I pursued fourteen years later was painfully dark, and I felt certain I would never be happy again.

My best friend's husband, Gary, was reeling in his own grief after his wife's death, quietly trying to process it with his two boys, both in their formative years when every young boy needs the care and nurture of a mother. It seemed like a good solution to have his two kids get together with my two kids, who stairstepped his boys in age.

Gary's work required a lengthy commute, so I pitched in to manage school transport and extracurricular activities. We began to have the occasional dinner out with all six of us, and that gradually grew into Gary and I talking over the phone in the evenings. Spiritually, we were in two very different places. I had been raised in church, and Gary had terminated his mandated childhood attendance at Catholic Mass as soon as he was able.

I had always considered myself close to God, but the divorce stoked my anger at him. I had prayed for years for my husband and felt those prayers had fallen on deaf ears, leaving me feeling abandoned. I reached a breaking point one evening and railed at God. "I don't even know if you're real, but if you are, you better show up now or I'm done!" My phone, which I had thrown through the wall only moments earlier in my rage, rang as soon as I yelled those words. Through tears I answered, and a friend of twelve years on the other end of the line assured me that God had put me on her heart for two days, and when it became too urgent to ignore, she had relented and called. I had felt so alone, but God had providentially answered my call for help through a friend who was oblivious to the circumstances of the moment.

This unexpected answer to prayer impacted my growing relationship with Gary. We began to talk about God and his pursuit of people. We spent hours discussing this subject. One evening, Gary asked me out on a date. I had been deeply touched by his kindness, his openness to truth, his generosity with his time, his patience with the kids, and his gentleness with everyone. In one short year we were married.

Looking back, the odds did not look to be in our favor. I was an angry mess and didn't realize how much of my internalized anger wouldn't stay compartmentalized within the framework of a previous marriage. I unknowingly carried it into my new marriage with Gary. Additionally, we were raising four grief-stricken tweens. Doors slammed, kids yelled, tempers flared.

I knew the answers our family needed were in God, so I threw myself into Bible study, and Gary and I continued to have those deep discussions about God's pursuit of us. One Saturday a few years later, Gary set up a date for us . . . to get baptized. That shift was so big, I'm surprised I didn't feel the earth move. Even though we still faced challenges, we were on a different path, a better path, together and with God.

For the first time that we recognized, we experienced God's love and his desire to partner with us, and we finally knew our identity was in this cooperation with him. During those few years of grief, loss, transition, and rediscovering, I learned what it meant to run to God, to throw everything at his feet, including my guilt, shame, and regret, and let him carry the weight of betrayal, despair, depression, and loneliness. When my first marriage ended, I wasn't sure I'd ever be happy again, but now I look to God for my joy, to be the lifter of my head. My identity comes from what God says about me, not from how well I can live up to others' expectations.

For over a decade now, Gary and I have been ministering to others struggling with life's difficulties, primarily in premarital and marital counseling, seeking to illuminate a path to healing through a deeper relationship with God. If we'd been told twenty-seven years ago that this was where God would lead us, we probably would have laughed. God has taken our pain and grief and our transformed understanding of our identity in him and turned everything around for our good, his glory, and service to others.

God's Perspective of Our Identity

God always views us as the much-loved products of his creation, while we tend to look at ourselves through the lens of our failures and our painful, broken, mixed-up pasts. The Bible offers many accounts of God helping his servants understand their true identity. Moses felt inadequate to speak to God's people, so God reminded Moses that he was going with him and that God would speak for him. Despite Abraham and Sarah's sin, God changed their names and in doing so offered them a more accurate perception of their identity in him as the spiritual parents of many generations. When Saul became Paul, he no longer punished Christians but instead was punished for championing faith in Jesus Christ. The nameless woman with the issue of blood is the only one mentioned in Scripture as being called "daughter" by Jesus.

Often, the enemy uses the pain from our past, whether self-inflicted or not, to color our perception of who we are. Even unknowingly, we adopt the labels perpetuated by society—cancer patient, barren, divorcée, prisoner, ex-friend, etc.—and live in the shadows of a life we wished we had prior to the pain we endured. But God never defines us or our identity by our pain; instead, he uses our pain to move, to shape, to teach, to transform us and our relationship with him.

In Western culture, when we break a household item, like a plate or a vase, we tend to throw it away, discarding it for something new, better, complete, and unbroken. We tend to do that with our past pain as well, trying to forget it as we move toward something new, better, complete, and unbroken.

What if we would trust God to take our brokenness and create something beautiful?

But what if we would trust God to take our brokenness and create something beautiful?

You might be familiar with the Japanese concept of kintsugi, the practice of taking broken pottery and "mending" it with a glue-like lacquer mixed with powdered gold, silver, or platinum. This practice honors the history of the object, highlighting the brokenness as something to be displayed with great respect and worth rather than hiding it. God honors our pain and considers our scars sacred. He brings good that we could never have anticipated out of our pain.

In my most painful trials, several verses strengthened me as I walked forward not knowing how God would use my pain for good.

> The Spirit of the Sovereign LORD is on me,
> because the LORD has anointed me
> to proclaim good news to the poor.
> He has sent me to bind up the brokenhearted,
> to proclaim freedom for the captives
> and release from darkness for the prisoners,
> to proclaim the year of the LORD's favor
> and the day of vengeance of our God,
> to comfort all who mourn,
> and provide for those who grieve in Zion—
> to bestow on them a crown of beauty
> instead of ashes,
> the oil of joy
> instead of mourning,

> and a garment of praise
> > instead of a spirit of despair.
> They will be called oaks of righteousness,
> > a planting of the Lord
> > for the display of his splendor. (Isa. 61:1–3)

Satan wants us to hide our pain and brokenness in defeat and shame, while God wants to celebrate the progress we've made and the healing he's shaped in his effort to bring beauty from the ashes of our pain-filled lives.

To heal from our painful past, whether that pain is physical, emotional, relational, or spiritual, we must recognize our faulty thinking, then adopt God's perspective:

1. We may think we'll never change, but God declares **we are a new creation**. "This means that anyone who belongs to Christ has become a new person. The old life is gone; a new life has begun!" (2 Cor. 5:17 NLT).

2. We recognize we are sinners, but because of Jesus's sacrifice, **God declares us forgiven**. "I am writing to you, dear children, because your sins have been forgiven on account of his name" (1 John 2:12).

3. We may deem ourselves unlovable, but God says **we are forever loved**. "For I am convinced that neither death nor life, neither angels nor demons, neither the present nor the future, nor any powers, neither height nor depth, nor anything else in all creation, will be able to separate us from the love of God that is in Christ Jesus our Lord" (Rom. 8:38–39).

4. We may feel too weak for the task at hand, but God reminds us that **he makes us strong**. "It is God who arms me with strength and keeps my way secure" (Ps. 18:32).

5. We may think of ourselves as broken, but just like the beautiful kintsugi pottery, **God makes us whole**. "So you also are complete through your union with Christ, who is the head over every ruler and authority" (Col. 2:10 NLT).

6. Because of our past, we may feel abandoned, but in his great love, **God has adopted us**. "God decided in advance to adopt us into his own family by bringing us to himself through Jesus Christ. This is what he wanted to do, and it gave him great pleasure" (Eph. 1:5 NLT).

7. Our own past, or even the actions of others toward us, may leave us feeling hopeless, especially when God seems slow to answer our prayers, but as long as God is on his throne, **we can remain hopeful**. "'For I know the plans I have for you,' declares the LORD, 'plans to prosper you and not to harm you, plans to give you hope and a future'" (Jer. 29:11).

8. We may feel worthless, but God says **Jesus died because we are worth it**. "For God so loved the world that he gave his one and only Son, that whoever believes in him shall not perish but have eternal life" (John 3:16).

9. We may not feel special, but God says **we are intentionally, fearfully, and wonderfully made**. "I praise you because I am fearfully and wonderfully made; your works are wonderful, I know that full well" (Ps. 139:14).

10. We may dwell on our failures, but **God declares us victorious in Christ**. "But thanks be to God! He gives us the victory through our Lord Jesus Christ" (1 Cor. 15:57).

Dear friend, perhaps you are in a place of still waiting for your physical, emotional, relational, or spiritual healing to come. I've learned on this journey that as much as we want to, we can't rush our healing. It is a process, and it is largely governed by God, who knows what's best for us. And yet we can participate in that process and look to the One who is able to make all things new. I beg you not to isolate in shame but lean in with expectancy for how he's going to make all things new, bring purpose to your past, and bring beauty in exchange for your ashes of pain.

A Scarred Perspective

For the Lord GOD helps Me,
Therefore, I have not been ashamed *or* humiliated.
Therefore, I have made My face like flint,
And I know that I shall not be put to shame. (Isa. 50:7
   AMP, italics in original)

My Prayer for You

Father, you are not the author of shame, guilt, or regret but of mercy, grace, forgiveness, and redemption. Help this precious one give you their shame and the lies they've believed about their identity and adopt a fresh perspective consistent with what you say about them. You make all things new, including the sacred scars of their past. Thank you that you never waste what we go through as you help us to grow through it. In Jesus's name, amen.

Recommended Playlist

"OK," Josh Wilson, © 2018 by Black River
"What My Father Does," John Waller, © 2021 by Ground-
   work Records

FOUR

Feel It to Heal It

I know that the LORD will maintain the cause
of the afflicted,
and will execute justice for the needy.

Psalm 140:12 ESV

We often hear of violent crimes in the news and either gawk in fascination or astonishment or turn away because we don't want to vicariously feel the pain endured by the victim. My friend Lisa was one of those victims. You would never know it to look at her—she is beautiful, intelligent, well-spoken, and poised. Her story is one that I felt compelled to share not just because of the pain she experienced and the sacred scars she now bears but because it also underscores the importance of getting help to heal from our past pain when we might otherwise be tempted to shelve those hurtful memories, ignore them, and refrain from letting God bring his healing light into the darkness. Lisa's scars testify that we must feel the pain to heal it. Lisa shares:

———◼———

Eighteen: the age of becoming. It was the year that I first left home. I decided what I ate for dinner, what classes I took in college, what time I went to bed, and how I spent my free time. It was that gossamer-thin year when I transitioned from trusting child to confident adult. Eighteen was also the age that I learned that the world is not always a safe place.

I have many fond memories of my college years—great friends, fun times, and exciting achievements. But my freshman year also brought me to the deepest valley I could have imagined when I became the victim of a horrific violent crime that movies are made of. My confidence and excitement quickly turned to horror, terror, and uncertainty. The strong will that drove my mother crazy in my tween and teen years became the survival skill I most relied on. I was determined not to let one night of terror derail my plans or education. Because my attacker had worn a ski mask to hide his identity, no arrest would be made and no justice would be served. I consciously decided to put one foot in front of the other and never think of the incident again. I packed those memories securely away in a box and placed them on a back shelf in my brain like old photographs.

The problem with old, stored memories is that they never truly disappear. I discovered this fact thirty-five years later when I learned that the masked man had been identified. My cold case was reopened, and so was the box of memories I had so carefully hidden but never healed from.

"Hello?" I answered the phone that morning expecting it to be another telemarketer.

It was someone calling from the police department in the area where my attack had occurred. "We have a case we are working on and would like to talk with you about it."

When I heard the words, "They have found the man who attacked you," I was instantly eighteen years old again. It was as if the box of memories had been taken off the shelf and strewn in front of me. I pictured myself in the room where it happened, struggling to catch my breath, terrified, shaking, and fighting to stay alert and alive.

The shock was not short-lived. Over the next days, weeks, and months, I continued to flash back to the incident with such clarity that I felt transported back in time. The detailed memories surprised me. I remembered what I was wearing, what the room smelled like, the sound of his voice, and more. The memories I thought were locked away for good were well-preserved and vivid. I repeatedly woke up in the middle of the night feeling as if I were drowning, the same way I felt when the man had tried to suffocate me. One night my husband got into bed after I had fallen asleep, and I jumped out of bed screaming as my fight-or-flight response automatically kicked in.

I was embarrassed to admit that this was PTSD (post-traumatic stress disorder). I was a trauma therapist; shouldn't I have been immune to this? I was a Christian who led others in worship. I knew the power of God. Didn't I trust him enough to let go of those memories?

When I was eighteen, I avoided talking about the incident. I didn't trust others to help and support me. My coping strategy was to pretend like nothing had ever happened. I didn't realize it then, but that had been a big mistake.

When the case reopened, I finally sought godly counsel with a qualified psychologist. I shared my story with my family, some of whom had never known what happened to me. Most importantly, I grew in faith and trusted in God's healing love. I journaled daily and found that God responded in various intimate ways.

As my wounds began to heal, I also found my voice. Because of the details of my case, I began to receive calls from legislators and other stakeholders who wanted to create safer circumstances for survivors of sexual violence. Each call ended the same way: "Please consider writing a book to let others know about your experience."

I had never entertained the idea of writing a book. I knew I could write, but a whole book? No way. But write I did. God continued to open doors, and I continued to step through. He allowed me to talk with state legislators and members of Congress. He gave me the courage and confidence to confront powerful people about what they can do to help and their responsibility to help ensure more rights for victims than for perpetrators. In doing so, he fulfilled the commission in Proverbs 31:8–9: "Speak up for those who cannot speak for themselves, for the rights of all who are destitute. Speak up and judge fairly; defend the rights of the poor and needy."

God also opened doors for me to become a national speaker. I have spoken to Christian women's groups, at Christian retreats and conferences, on college campuses, and in churches, sharing God's message of healing. Although I never thought I would be a writer or speaker, God had other plans to use my pain for his glory.

Today I can see that, although God doesn't purpose for us to experience trauma in life, he can use all things for his purposes. I have learned that healing is possible, even when this world seems to offer no happy endings, and I have been able to share that message with many others who have experienced trauma and need healing. I am blessed to be able to comfort others with the same comfort I received from Jesus on my journey. In addition to writing and speaking, I continue to work as a trauma therapist. I now work almost solely with survivors of sexual violence, and I can confidently assure each that hope for healing is not futile. God heals, and the scars that remain are a beautiful reminder of his healing touch.

Lisa's story, like so many others told within these pages, is one that none of us would choose to endure. Yet we all will suffer some kind of pain, whether it be physical, emotional, relational, or spiritual. When we do something to contribute to our own pain, we often experience guilt with the nagging questions, *Why did I _____? What if I hadn't _____? Would things be different if only _____?* And yet when our pain comes at the hands or words of others, our tendency is often to strike out and blame, even if the only source we decide to blame is God.

And then our questions often turn to, *Where were you when this happened, God? Why didn't you prevent it? Don't you love or care about me, God?* I would imagine that if I put myself in Lisa's situation, I would have all those questions and more. There often aren't easy answers for our pain, but that's when it's crucial that we embrace what we know to be true from God's Word. Lisa's scars reflect her learning to rely on God to be her Advocate, Defender, Healer, and Comforter, and we must too. But in order for God to comfort and heal us, we have to feel the pain to heal it. Denial just prolongs the pain.

Consenting to Give Up the Pain

In our Western culture, the societal mantra has become, "If it's going to be, it's up to me." I lived that lie for too many years, striving to be all things to all people and taking on burdens that I was ill-equipped to carry, until my body raised the white flag of surrender. Rather than carrying all our pain, shame, guilt, regret, fear, and worry by ourselves, we are called to "give all your worries and cares to God, for he cares about you" (1 Pet. 5:7 NLT). But God doesn't take our cares without our consent—it is a matter of our will to hand them over to him and not pick them up again.

Enduring a violent crime, longing for a prodigal child to come home, digging out from bankruptcy, undergoing cancer treatment, or living through an extramarital affair are each too painful to carry by ourselves. The pain cuts deep, and the emotional wounds often cause a ripple effect in our attitudes and beliefs that can cause extensive collateral damage. God never intended for us to be capable of healing ourselves—that's why he promised to be our Healer.

> Praise the LORD, my soul,
>   and forget not all his benefits—

> who forgives all your sins
>> and heals *all* your diseases,
> who redeems your life from the pit
>> and crowns you with love and compassion,
> who satisfies your desires with good things
>> so that your youth is renewed like the eagle's.
>> (Ps. 103:2–5 emphasis added)

In this lifetime, where evil is fighting to keep as much control as possible, we can choose to despair and wish God would right all the wrong, or we can trust that he will execute justice in due time. God's very nature will not allow him to tolerate sin and evildoing. But our perspective of time is so skewed with a focus on the immediate that we lose sight of the fact that God's timing is perfect, and in the span of eternity, what we think of as so time-sensitive is but an almost imperceptible blip on God's timeline. We can get so focused on our desire for healing and justice that we lose sight of God. "But you must return to your God; maintain love and justice, and wait for your God always" (Hosea 12:6).

We can get so focused on our desire for healing and justice that we lose sight of God.

I remember going through a particularly tumultuous time many years ago and knowing that the pain cut so deep and my perception was so skewed because of it that I could not walk through my healing journey alone. I knew that the pain held me hostage, and I was concerned that if I didn't process the pain and God's path to healing with another qualified individual, I would become beholden to bitterness, resentment, and anger. I ventured approximately an hour away from home each week to work through my pain with a therapist who neither knew me previously nor was a source of referrals to my practice. Sometimes the best help we can find is that offered by an unbiased, qualified party.

As I sat in her office, on her couch, her eyes were soft but knowing. Her speech was measured, but she never hurried to jump in with an opinion or thought; instead, she allowed me time to both share my jagged heart and process my own words that had previously been unvoiced to another living soul. At some point, she encouraged, "Let it all out, Michelle. This is a safe place. You must feel it to heal it." That sounded like something I would say to my own patients, and that is a truism within the field of psychology. Yet I admitted, "I'm afraid to feel it, afraid to cry . . . I'm afraid if I open that door, I'll never be able to close the floodgates of tears I've choked down for years." And yet I knew she was right. When we don't take time to grieve, to feel the pain and acknowledge its disruption in our lives, we can't heal. At some point the volcano will erupt and the lava of pain will demand tending to, but unfortunately, it often comes when we're least expecting it and even less capable of dealing with it.

Keep Your Heart Tender

Friend, we must feel the pain to heal the pain. When we avoid it, we run the risk of our heart becoming hard, future experiences magnifying its existence, and skewing our perspective regarding ourselves, others, and the world around us. I'm a staunch advocate of good, quality mental health help by a qualified professional, but I also fully believe in God's ability to heal our bodies, minds, and hearts. God is a gentleman—he isn't going to wrestle us for control. He does his best work through a heart surrendered to him. "I will give you a new heart and put a new spirit in you; I will remove from you your heart of stone and give you a heart of flesh" (Ezek. 36:26). We don't want to carry around a heart of stone. First, it hurts us and makes it harder for us to sense the voice and will of God, but it also closes us off from the love, compassion, and fellowship of others.

Let's remember who the real enemy is: "For our struggle is not against flesh and blood, but against the rulers, against the authorities, against the powers of this dark world and against the spiritual forces of evil in the heavenly realms" (Eph. 6:12). Pain and suffering don't come from God, but the enemy will use them to isolate us, to shame us, and to distract us from the fullness of life that God has for us. The enemy counts on us not recognizing him and his ways and running away from pain, scared. So, when you experience it, instead of retreating in fear or defeat, recognize the work of our enemy. Turn your mind and heart toward God in prayer and praise and seek out companionship with other believers. Sometimes it's hard for us to allow ourselves to go into the dark dungeon of pain in our heart, because we long for justice, and we desire for God to defend us. We can be assured that that day is coming.

In Lisa's situation above, she went decades without any answers regarding who her perpetrator was, much less any hope for justice. Yet, often the best justice that we can have is to live joyful, contented lives despite the pain we've endured. No one would ever willingly choose to go through what Lisa endured on that college campus as a young adult woman, and her pain was so crushing that she attempted to forget. But our bodies keep the score, and our minds remember on some level. With help, she received her healing and is now working to help ensure the healing of countless other victims—something that could only be accomplished with God's help, and her willing heart.

> **Often the best justice that we can have is to live joyful, contented lives despite the pain we've endured.**

Taking Our Discouragement to God

In the Old Testament book of Jeremiah, we find an example of an individual who had to "feel it to heal it." Jeremiah endured frequent wounding: physical, familial, social, and relational. To do his job as a prophet to God's people in a very stressful time of their history, Jeremiah had to manage buckets of pain and had only one place to turn.

God had called Jeremiah from the time he was in the womb. His whole life was spent in prophetic work. But God indicated that the people would fight against Jeremiah and not accept God's words through him, like they had done with Isaiah. Jeremiah's call from God included these words:

> "Today I have made you a fortified city, an iron pillar and a bronze wall to stand against the whole land—against the kings of Judah, its officials, its priests and the people of the land. They will fight against you but will not overcome you, for I am with you and will rescue you," declares the LORD. (Jer. 1:18–19)

This sounds like a pretty good clue that the work would be tough.

During his lifetime of prophecy, Jeremiah suffered a conspiracy on his life from his own family, imprisonment multiple times, beatings, public humiliation, and abandonment in a muddy cistern to die. He was opposed by powerful people from the king's court and from the priesthood. He was accused of being a traitor, a false prophet, and harmful to the morale of the people. He repeatedly prophesied disaster from the north, a prophecy that came true with the sacking of Jerusalem by Babylon, but only several decades after he started prophesying. That event was preceded by an eighteen-month siege resulting in famine and disease within the city. Jeremiah was witness to what he had prophesied and the horror, death, and destruction that attended it. Jeremiah is called 'the weeping prophet" because of his message of destruction to a people who would not accept it and the grief he felt personally.

Although Jeremiah had the promise of God's rescue, support, and strength, he still suffered humanly. In chapter 20, Jeremiah vents his emotions to God:

> O LORD, you misled me,
>   and I allowed myself to be misled.
> You are stronger than I am,
>   and you overpowered me.
> Now I am mocked every day;
>   everyone laughs at me.
> When I speak, the words burst out.
>   "Violence and destruction!" I shout.
> So these messages from the LORD
>   have made me a household joke.
> But if I say I'll never mention the LORD
>   or speak in his name,
> his word burns in my heart like a fire.
>   It's like a fire in my bones!
> I am worn out trying to hold it in!
>   I can't do it!
> I have heard the many rumors about me.
>   They call me "The Man Who Lives in Terror."
> They threaten, "If you say anything, we will report it."
>   Even my old friends are watching me,
>   waiting for a fatal slip.
> "He will trap himself," they say,
>   "and then we will get our revenge on him."
>   (vv. 7–10 NLT)

Jeremiah complains of being misled and that he hadn't expected his prophetic work to be so difficult, but he also recognizes his own naivete about it. He insinuates that God "forced" him into the work he's doing (so, he's blaming God) but is also clear that he cannot *not* speak, that he can't hold in the words God gives him (v. 9). He knows that his message is unpopular and repetitive, and he reflects on being mocked, laughed at, and made a joke of. Finally, he reports the attitude of others, including old friends, who are waiting for him to slip or fail, to get revenge on him.

Elsewhere and at another time, Jeremiah complains to God:

> Why is my pain unending
>   and my wound grievous and incurable?
> You are to me like a deceptive brook,
>   like a spring that fails. (Jer. 15:18)

These are two of several excerpts from the book that highlight Jeremiah's personal struggles with the message he was delivering and the pain and suffering that attended it (see also Jer. 11:18–12:6; 15:10–21; 17:14–18; 18:18–23). He did not withhold his frustration with God, painting evocative word pictures of how he perceived his Maker and the One who promised to support him.

The book of Jeremiah is not his personal journal, and his personal feelings were never his primary concern, even when he was willing to record them. The book itself is not particularly chronological in sequence, so we can't really trace the trajectory of Jeremiah's responses to his sufferings and wounds. We can, however, see some of the verses that accompanied his laments. Immediately following the section of chapter 20 that we just looked at is this:

> But the LORD is with me like a mighty warrior;
>   so my persecutors will stumble and not prevail.

They will fail and be thoroughly disgraced;
    their dishonor will never be forgotten.
Lord Almighty, you who examine the righteous
    and probe the heart and mind,
let me see your vengeance on them,
    for to you I have committed my cause.

Sing to the Lord!
    Give praise to the Lord!
He rescues the life of the needy
    from the hands of the wicked. (vv. 11–13)

The book of Jeremiah is full of phrases like "The Lord replied . . ." or "The Lord revealed . . ." or "The Lord said to me . . ." It appears that Jeremiah was very active in his relationship with God. He was quick to both praise God and lament to him, forthrightly and in detail. He recognized his own limitations, and readily made his requests, both personally and for the people. One wonders if Jeremiah's "journey to healing" from the suffering he endured as an unpopular and outspoken presence in the culture was simply this active relationship, and whether the horrifying things we read about in his life that we find significant or scary simply became the next things he talked to God about.

Despite the public vitriol, Jeremiah was a counselor to kings. He was recognized by the Babylonian conquerors as an effective leader and was offered the option of staying or traveling to Babylon. He survived the tongue-lashings and the whip lashings, the prison cells, and the muddy cistern. In his recorded laments, Jeremiah didn't use the language of healing; he did not focus on his suffering or ask God for respite from it. Instead, Jeremiah used the language of relationship; he recognized that God functioned as his Advocate, Defender, and Deliverer. Jeremiah knew that directly from the mouth of God himself (see

Jer. 1:8, 18–19; 11:18; 12:6; and 20:11), and he availed himself of God's willingness to adopt these roles in his life.

Friend, I don't know what painful trial you currently face or what you've previously walked through, but my prayer is that you will feel the pain in order to heal it. I pray that you will take your pain to God and let him be your Advocate, Defender, Healer, and Comforter. Sometimes for healing to begin, it looks like letting go, surrendering the pain for the healing on the other side.

Let me encourage you:

Let it go . . . the offense.

Let it go . . . the pain.

Let it go . . . the right to be right.

Let it go . . . the argument.

Let it go . . . the dream of what should have been.

Let it go . . . the bitterness.

Let it go . . . the resentment.

Let it go . . . the unforgiveness.

Let it go . . . the desire for revenge.

Let it go . . . the vindication.

Let it go . . . the shame.

Let it go . . . the guilt.

Let it go . . . the regret.

Jesus already paid the price for you to live in freedom. Don't let the pain hold you hostage anymore. In exchange for your pain, God wants to give you good things because he loves you (see James 1:17), and he has a plan for you filled with hope and a future (see Jer. 29:11). Will you hold his hand and allow yourself to feel it so you can heal it?

A Scarred Perspective

Therefore he is able to save completely those who come to God through him, because he always lives to intercede for them. (Heb. 7:25)

My Prayer for You

Father, at times our pain and suffering seem too much to bear. This was never intended to be your way, and yet you always make a way for us to endure. Would you help the one reading these words now carry their pain to you for you to take from them? Help them to acknowledge the pain and then trust in you to heal every wound. Let their scars be a testimony of the healing you provided that will strengthen their fortitude and faith before the next trial descends on the landscape of their life. In Jesus's name, amen.

Recommended Playlist

"Show Me Where You Were," Laney Rene, © 2022 by Laney Rene Music

"For the Good," Riley Clemmons, © 2021 by Capitol CMG, Inc.

"The Heat," Lola Bliss, © 2023 by Lola Bliss

"It's Not Over," Mandisa, Jasmine Murray, and Rita Springer, © 2020 by Capitol CMG, Inc.

"Honest," Kyndal Inskeep, © 2022 by Song House

FIVE

Scars Can Deepen Our Walk with God

> One thing I ask from the LORD,
>   this only do I seek:
> that I may dwell in the house of the LORD
>   all the days of my life,
> to gaze on the beauty of the LORD
>   and to seek him in his temple.
>
> Psalm 27:4

Pain and suffering are inevitable, but we choose how we cope with them. I was born into a family with a mother who suffered from severe depression and modeled looking at life through a negative, depressed, glass-completely-empty lens. As a result, I had to learn to intentionally choose to look at life through a shifted, more positive, and God-honoring perspective. God blessed me greatly when he gifted me with my husband and his parents as part of my new family. They are three of the most positive, optimistic people you could meet.

Their positivity has never presented as being Pollyannaish or a denial of the truth but rather a gratitude for all God has blessed them with and a refusal to live in the what-ifs of life. Instead, they have a "Thank you for _____" perspective.

Having been married to Scott for over thirty-five years, I know the devastating circumstances my husband has endured and the grace with which he has walked through pain. Scott's story reflects the truth that our scars can deepen our walk with God, and I asked him to share it with you from his perspective:

———■———

It has been almost a quarter of a century since the events of my first cancer diagnosis and treatment. Much has changed, but my scar remains. It runs from the bottom of my ribcage to my pelvis, right through where my belly button used to be.

My original diagnosis came in an after-hours phone call from my doctor himself (that's rarely a good sign!). I recall little of the conversation other than I was standing outside watching the sunset. The doctor ended our call by saying, "I'm sorry, Mr. Bengtson. You're too young for this." The first oncologist we visited literally used the phrase "Get your affairs in order." I thought that was only a Hollywood thing. It's not. I made the mistake of asking for a prognosis. Two years. Two short years. After that appointment, Michelle and I sat in the parking lot and cried. We were still young, still considered ourselves newly-weds, were new parents, and up until that diagnosis, thought we had decades ahead of us, together.

We providentially became acquainted with a second oncologist, who was a specialist in an unusual surgical technique for my rare form of cancer and was so new in town that he answered his own phone when we called for an appointment. Treatment was intrusive, inconvenient, recurrent, and fear-inducing, at least in the beginning. It began with major surgery tied to a nontrivial chance of dying on the table. I was literally unconscious, but Michelle endured a twenty-three-hour, edge-of-her-seat waiting-room experience, uncertain of the outcome and jumping up every time medical personnel came through the door.

Treatment progressed according to plan: surgery, ICU recovery, four months of homebound recovery, port placement for chemo, and a nine-month routine of weekly chemotherapy. Close friends and family members rotated in and out of our home, trying to help us with daily activities and childcare while I was unable to do much other than rest and recover. While I was getting kudos for bravery and being held up as an example of endurance, I had a much more passive perspective: "I'm just the patient following the plan. What else would I do?"

Throughout this time, though, and for years afterward, I was anxious about an expected relapse, about losing this life and my family, which had seemingly been snatched away only to be returned under a cloud. The disease was slow-moving, which made it hard to treat and even more difficult to ensure it was gone. My trepidation built as every regular checkup date approached, first monthly, then quarterly, then semiannually, then annually. I still find myself more tense before a checkup and notably relieved afterward.

I grew up with a strong sense of God's sovereignty and presence in this world, but I really only understood this in a childlike way, maybe because much of what I learned came from those formative growing-up years. My Sunday school teachers frequently used a set of paper-cutout figures mounted on flannel as visuals, with the endearingly descriptive name of flannelgraphs. This was the PowerPoint of the 1960s. By my teen years, I had a reasonable grasp on theology, but my God remained a paper-cutout figure.

My illness, treatment, and enduring uncertainty of recurrence incinerated my paper-cutout vision of God. Although my exposure to strong theology provided a robust cognitive understanding, it didn't help me live it. It didn't offer the practical things that let me respond to the knocks that come in life, especially the one that came that year and echoed through the following decades.

Over those years, that incinerated paper-cutout God miraculously came alive. He gently enabled me to recognize the existential angst that came from that experience, the question that loomed behind every conversation and every thought—*Will I live?* As I walked through life in the continued presence of this question, three activities—none of which I anticipated—shifted the question. Instead of the angst and despair of *Will I live?* the question slowly changed to *How will I live?* These activities were not coincident with my diagnosis and treatment. They mostly occurred slowly and irregularly, and I can't directly link them to my terrible, no good, rotten health experience. But the contrast in my perspective was stark and definitive. These three activities were worship, prayer, and my routine exposure to God's Word in the company of a small group of like-minded men.

I perceived worship in my youth to be dull and uninspiring, but coming out of my health experience, I began to see worship as connected to my relationship with God. It articulated something I could not put into my own words but that I found to be powerfully true, and it captured in song the eternal and unchanging but always novel and relational character of God. It described my life, with its fears, angst, hopes, and distractions. This changing perspective on worship required little personal initiative. I just showed up Sunday morning. But I also began to recognize that worship was an opportunity and that I didn't go to church to worship, but rather I brought my worship to church.

My prayers during that time were the most desperate of my life. They reflected my state of mind—fragile, doubtful, fearful, irregular, and very focused on my own sense of loss and grief. During my time of emotional and physical tenuousness, God reflected to me a constancy that was comforting. He promised no miraculously quick and positive resolution, but he remained present. Many years later, a psalm captured my experience, and it comforts me still today: "When my anxious thoughts multiply within me, Your consolations delight my soul" (Ps. 94:19 NASB1995). Many nights I have drifted back to sleep with this on my mind after waking in a dark worry. I gained a deeper understanding that this living, active, and present God was a good and abundant God. My prayers became less about vocalizing some existential concern and more about reflecting on God's presence and participation in my life. Despite the specter of death and loss, he still provides and offers peace and abundance; the greatest gift, however, is that of his constant presence.

Shortly after my initial diagnosis and treatment, I started participating with a small group of men who wanted to open the Bible and know God better. During our weeks of discussion, I came to realize that Jesus was not just a paper cutout. He was a man who experienced the joys and travails of life like I do. The head knowledge of God that I had acquired was good, but it took continuous and serious exposure to the Word of God to put muscles to those bones.

After the leader moved away and that original group disbanded, I stepped into the role as leader of a new group of men, knowing that would encourage me to regularly study the Bible with the aim of experiencing a deeper relationship with God. God's presence in my life is now more real than it has ever been, even surpassing the reality of the physical world around me.

My wounds have healed, and my scars have faded over time, as have the visceral memories of the disease, surgery, chemotherapy, and concerns of recurrence, but the lessons learned have not dimmed. Doctors forecasted my death, but God gave life—an abundant life walking hand in hand in a personal relationship with Jesus, no longer a cutout version of him. He extends the opportunity for friendship with him to you today as well, so that you don't have to face your pain alone. He is ever present and offers friendship with all who will "come near," as James says. "Come near to God and he will come near to you" (4:8).

When Pain Continues

In *The Hem of His Garment*, we talked about the different kinds of pain: physical, emotional, relational, financial, spiritual, grief, and even secondary pain inflicted by others that complicates our preexisting pain. When pain continues longer than we believe ourselves capable of tolerating, we often wonder, *Where are you when I hurt, God? Do you see me? Do you even care that I am suffering?* I've been there. Sometimes in our darkest valleys, God seems the quietest, and the enemy will use that to instill doubt regarding God's presence and whether we can trust God when he says he will never leave us or forsake us (see Deut. 31:6).

God didn't create us for pain and suffering, but he can use it for our good. God never wastes our pain.

God didn't create us for pain and suffering, but he can use it for our good. God never wastes our pain, although we may not see his hand in our suffering until we receive some healing and scars begin to form.

In *The Hem of His Garment*, Job was a frequent topic of conversation. Job—the man who was blameless and upright before the Lord and yet the man on whom God allowed Satan to inflict every kind of pain and suffering. I cannot imagine losing my livelihood, my household, my children, and my health successively, with no time to heal or recover in between. Job's misguided friends blamed him for much of his misery, adding relational and secondary pain to the financial, physical, and spiritual pain he already endured. Job listened to and managed their criticism for much longer than I could have, until he finally struck out and began asking God, "Why?" With the scabs of his losses being fresh and swollen and his heart yearning for life as it was before, he couldn't see a purpose for his pain or a path through it. God didn't respond immediately, and when he finally offered his wisdom to Job, he didn't answer the question, "Why?" Instead, God provided the answers to the more important questions that Job probably should have been asking: *Who are you, God? What does my suffering say about you? What do you want me to learn from this experience? And how will you work even this tragedy for my good?*

I've asked those questions. I've never found it helpful to ask why pain and suffering have occurred. It wouldn't make me feel any better to know why someone abused a child, why a spouse had an extramarital affair, why a murderer randomly chose a victim, or why cancer took the life of someone I loved. It would do nothing to minimize the pain and likely cause me to become angry because the answer would be insufficient to justify the suffering. God didn't answer Job's question, "Why?" Instead, he revealed more of himself to Job, just as he did to Scott throughout his cancer experience and subsequent treatment journey and as he has done so often for me.

We will never fully appreciate the limitlessness of God until we cross through the veil into glory. God spent a couple of chapters listing his résumé to Job, impressing upon him Job's very limited understanding of the vastness of God. Through his pain and suffering, Job grew closer to God as his grasp of God increased. "My ears had heard of you, but now my eyes have seen you. Therefore I despise myself and repent in dust and ashes" (Job 42:5–6). The answer to Job's questions no longer concerned him because his suffering yielded an intimate appreciation and understanding of God that he could have gleaned in no other way.

In our humanness, pain often prompts us to question God, to question his purpose and his plan, to question his character. *If I hurt, is God still good? If God allowed this suffering in my life, can he be trusted?* Job's story makes clear that God does not despise our doubt, our fears, and our questions. He welcomes the communication. But Job's account reveals that God is often more concerned with bringing us into a deeper relationship with him, and a greater appreciation of who he is, than he is with answering our specific questions. Friend, if we gain nothing more through our painful trials and suffering than a greater understanding of who God is and appreciate a deeper, more intimate relationship with him through it, we remain blessed indeed. Deepening our relationship with God comes through learning how much he loves us, that he would send Jesus to be the sacrifice for our sins and allow him to bleed and die on our behalf.

How Do You Relate to God?

In recent years, I've related most to God as my Healer (Jehovah Rapha, see Exod. 15:26) because that's what I've felt I needed most. But I've sensed that in the waiting, he's wanted to be—and is—more than that for me, and he wants to be more than that for you as well.

He is also:

Jehovah Rohi: Our Good Shepherd (see Ps. 23)—He is the One who guides and directs us and keeps us safe.

Jehovah Shalom: Our Prince of Peace (see Judg. 6:24)—He is the One who keeps our heart in peace when the troubles and cares threaten to overtake us with worry, anxiety, disappointment, pain, and discouragement.

Jehovah Shammah: Our Ever Present One ("the Lord is there"; see Ezek. 48:35)—He is the One who is with us in the difficult hours when the enemy tries to convince us we are all alone.

Jehovah Tsidkenu: Our Righteousness (see Jer. 23:6)—He is the One who defends us when the enemy accuses us before God in the courtroom of heaven.

Jehovah Nissi: The Lord is Our Banner; Our Battle Fighter (see Exod. 17:15)—He is the One who is willing to fight (and win) our battles when we are weary and battle worn.

Jehovah Jireh: Our Provider (see Gen. 22:14)—He is the
One who provides from the unlimited storehouses
of heaven when our own resources are limited and
insufficient.

And so much more. God is our Creator, our Father, our Advocate, our Strength, our Defender, our Comfort, our Shelter, our Rock, our Redeemer, our Savior, and our Friend. What would you add to that list?

We can get so shortsighted by our immediate needs that we lose track of the fact that we serve a more-than-enough, abundant God who is not limited by space or time or finances. When God declared, "I AM," he was declaring that he would not be put in a box, for he is *all* that we could ever need him to be. In his sovereignty, he knows when we need his comfort, his direction, and his safety, whereas at other times we might need him to be our Redeemer and our Restorer. Still other times, what we need most is that he be our Daddy, our Defender, and our Protector. So, today, let's invite him into our day, into our life, to be "I AM," all that he knows we need him to be. What do you need God to be for you today?

A Scarred Perspective

My ears had heard of you
  but now my eyes have seen you. (Job 42:5)

My Prayer for You

Father, you never waste our pain. Please use the pain of this one's past to draw them into a closer relationship

79

with you. Draw them into your arms to experience a fresh encounter of who you want to be for them. If deepening our relationship with you is the only positive thing to come out of our pain, it is enough, and we welcome it. In Jesus's name, amen.

Recommended Playlist

"Valley," Chris McClarney, © 2019 by Jesus Culture

"Somebody," ZOE Music, © 2020 by ZOE LA/Watershed

"You Know Me," Bethel Music, © 2012 by Bethel Music

"New Creation," Mac Powell, © 2021 by Mac Powell Records

"When Nothing Hurts," Riley Clemmons, © 2021 by Capitol CMG, Inc.

SIX

God Is Good and Faithful

Let us hold unswervingly to the hope we profess, for he who promised is faithful.

Hebrews 10:23

Those who bear scars from significant, life-threatening experiences almost always change because of the suffering they endured. Some become bitter; others allow their experiences and the lessons they've learned to help them become better. My friend Gina is the latter. I hope her story will encourage you to remain steadfast in the conviction that even when God allows bad things to happen to good people, he is still good, he is still faithful, and he redeems our painful past for our good and his glory. Here's a glimpse into Gina's story:

My life drastically changed on February 22, 1979, when I was eleven years old. As a sixth grader, I served one week a month as crossing guard for my elementary school. I embraced the responsibility as I donned my bright orange crossing-guard safety harness, complete with a reflective strip. We had no school buses in the district at that time. Either you walked or someone drove you to and from school. My mother waited approximately ten minutes after she saw me and the "walkers" pass by the school before driving to my assigned street corner to pick me up after I completed my duties. That was our routine. Yet that Thursday was far from routine.

I remember looking both ways prior to crossing the street, but I do not remember seeing the large, red pickup truck that struck me when I was only a few feet from the safety of the other side. The doctors surmised I must have been hit on the "up stride" of my running pattern. I was thrown nearly one hundred feet, landing in a snowbank on the side of the road. If I had been on the downward part of my running stride, I likely would have been crushed underneath the vehicle. I was the only one injured. My mom and younger brother came upon my accident before the ambulance arrived.

I sustained a significant closed head injury, or a "skull fracture," as it was explained to me as a child. I bore injury to the cranial nerves that control hearing and facial movement on the right side, leaving that side of my face paralyzed. I could not close my eye completely and could not move any muscles on that side of my face. I also incurred total loss of hearing in my right ear. Six ribs were broken, also on the right side, and my right lung collapsed.

Our small local hospital transferred me to a larger hospital with a neurosurgeon better able to care for my injuries. My brother stayed with a neighbor as my parents followed the ambulance to the hospital. Smart phones and Bible apps didn't exist at that time, but in my dad's pocket, he carried a small booklet with promises from God's Word. My parents clung to the promises they read. In the initial hours, doctors prepared them for the possibility that I might not live. They were cautioned that I might have significant brain damage and be unable to walk or talk again.

God cradled me in his arms as I lay broken in the hospital. Bravery didn't describe me; I leaned more toward shy and self-conscious. But I loved God and knew he loved me. Only years later did I learn the doctors did not expect me to live. And yet I remember telling my parents that I knew I would be all right.

I remain deaf in my right ear. I possess residual facial weakness that leaves me with a crooked smile and the ability to raise only one eyebrow when perplexed or scared. My middle back is stiff where the ribs healed and scar tissue formed, leaving me with less mobility in my spine than normal.

God used my experience as a child to lead me to become a pediatric physical therapist. When I show my patients the scar behind my right ear and my crooked smile, I have a bit of "street cred" with those children and their parents because scars attest to what I've survived.

For years I thought God's purpose for my accident might have been to enable me to share with others that he is good, faithful, and able to protect us in miraculous ways. I viewed my right-sided deafness and facial weakness as a type of memorial to the faithfulness of God. I have shared with others how God worked in my life. God has deepened my understanding of how specific his love and care is for us, especially as we are willing to share our scarred experiences with others.

Forty-four years later, I've learned my purpose is so much bigger than me. God did not save my life just for me to grow and know him better, although I have grown and have a deeper knowledge of God because of that day in '79. God taught me about his love, hope, compassion, goodness, and faithfulness and helps me use my scars to reveal his love, hope, and care to others.

I had never personally known another family who experienced an accident like mine until a few years ago when God gave me the opportunity to meet and comfort two sisters who had been hit by a car and required hospitalization. I want these two young precious friends to see themselves not as scarred and different from their peers but as their heavenly Father sees them: beautiful, strong, and loved. I want to walk alongside them, their parents, and their siblings, cheering them into the fullness of all that God has for them. I want to see God use their scars—yes, the hard things these beautiful and strong little girls have endured—to change their lives and the lives of those around them. I hope to take them one day to the spot where my accident occurred, to pray, with their family at my side, over that sacred spot in the road, right across from the Utz potato chip store in the town where I grew up. Healing comes as we invite Jesus into the places where we have been wounded. Healing is most deeply felt as we share our sacred scars with each other.

My sacred scars reflect God's goodness and faithfulness to me and my family. God can redeem any pain we've endured, but he offers us the opportunity to partner with him to share the lessons we've learned with others so that they can also experience a touch of God's goodness, faithfulness, and redemption.

The In-Between Stage

What do we do when we're in that in-between stage—hurting and longing for answers but without the perspective that comes with time and God's wisdom? Psalm 102 offers some insight. Uniquely, in the Psalter, Psalm 102 is titled with the description of a difficult situation but no notes on authorship or the historical context. The title reads, "A prayer of an afflicted person who has grown weak and pours out a lament before the LORD." The opening verses capture the sense of this in-between stage:

> Hear my prayer, LORD;
> let my cry for help come to you.
> Do not hide your face from me
> when I am in distress.
> Turn your ear to me;
> when I call, answer me quickly. (vv. 1–2)

We've all had those prolonged periods when we question the reason behind our suffering and even God's hand in it. *God,*

I know you are good, but why did you allow this to happen? God, why haven't you done what I know you have the power to do? What good can come out of this devastation?

Abraham and Sarah experienced a lot of "in-between." Their story encourages us to trust God's goodness and faithfulness even when we cannot see his hand at work or find answers for our questions.

Imagine being asked to break ties with your family, give up your inheritance, move to a foreign country, and change your faith from the dominant and familiar polytheistic religion to a strange monotheistic belief. Additionally, you marry a barren woman, nullifying your chance to create the family heritage that's a primary mark of cultural status. After you arrive where your strange God has led you, you endure a drought and famine, so you must keep moving to Egypt, another strange land. There, the king finds your seventy-five-year-old wife desirable, thinking she's available since you misleadingly described her as your sister, and takes her into his harem. He's cursed for this by your strange new God but returns your wife to you, then throws you out of Egypt instead of killing you.

Now imagine you return to the land your God originally brought you to, but there is war among several local states. Your nephew and his family are kidnapped by one faction, so you take your three hundred plus household servants and rescue them. The strange God you now follow promises you an heir, but you must wait fifteen years, even though you are already eighty-five years old. Growing tired of waiting for a child, your wife convinces you to sleep with her maidservant, which produces a child out of wedlock and predictable intra-family friction. Heaping pain on an already difficult history, when the promised child finally borne by your wife is about fifteen years old, God comes to you again and asks you to give the child up, to sacrifice him on an altar, to kill him. If I gave you this storyline without context, you might think it was a plot from a Netflix serial. This was Abraham's life for decades.

Abraham's scars serve as examples to us today. It is reasonable to think that he felt emotional wounds from leaving his family, his culture, and his inheritance. He was clearly troubled enough to flee the drought in Canaan and lie about his wife. Did he experience guilt and shame when his deception was discovered? He was near physical violence and witnessed the destruction of Sodom and Gomorrah (see Gen. 19:28), almost losing his nephew Lot and Lot's family. Did he fear for himself or his family? Abraham despaired enough for an heir that he brought it to God's attention (see Gen. 15:2–6), yet he exiled Hagar, his wife's servant, and her child to the wilderness. What cognitive or emotional pressures brought this to pass?

Yet in all this, Abraham found God's faithful presence and relied on his good provision. God initiated relationship with Abraham in calling him out of the land of his forefathers. God walked with Abraham and protected him to and through Canaan, into Egypt and back, and elsewhere. God blessed Abraham and allowed Abraham's name to be linked to his own (see Gen. 14:19). God provided the heir that Abraham treasured but also tested Abraham by asking him to sacrifice Isaac. Abraham's response was simply to believe God, trusting that he was good and faithful. Abraham acted accordingly, and Genesis records instances of Abraham building altars as impromptu places of worship and reminders of God's goodness and faithfulness.

Except for Moses, no other Old Testament hero is mentioned more in the New Testament than Abraham, and yet his life was far from perfect, and many of his personal choices were flawed. Abraham experienced repeated failure, but he believed God, and God honored this belief. He blessed Abraham, provided for him, protected him, and was present with him (see chaps. 11–25), even during Abraham's in-between stages.

Waiting for a New Perspective

In the middle of a painful experience, it can be hard to see God's good and faithful hand in our situation. It's a bit like trying to see a completed jigsaw puzzle when only the edges have been fit together or trying to see mountain vistas when we haven't yet left base camp. Authentic faith trusts God's character and what we know to be true about God when our circumstances try to convince us otherwise. God asks us to trust him—that he is good and that he is faithful to see us through, even before the pages turn on our painful story. "Being confident of this, that he who began a good work in you will carry it on to completion until the day of Christ Jesus" (Phil. 1:6).

Our sacred scars reflect God's faithfulness to bring us through our painful trials, but when we're still healing and the scars are yet to be formed, we need to remember those times that God was faithful in the past as well as his promise of new mercies when we need them today. In his reflection on the horrific destruction of Jerusalem and dismemberment of his country and culture, the Old Testament prophet Jeremiah wrote, "Because of the LORD's great love we are not consumed, for his compassions never fail. They are new every morning; great is your faithfulness" (Lam. 3:22–23).

> **Authentic faith trusts God's character and what we know to be true about God when our circumstances try to convince us otherwise.**

We often want God to prove his goodness and faithfulness by answering our prayers in a certain way, eliminating our pain, or providing justice for our situation on our timeline. God described himself to Moses as "The LORD, The LORD God, merciful and gracious, longsuffering, and abundant in goodness and truth" (Exod. 34:6 KJV). God proves his goodness and faithfulness not by paving an easy path through life but by walking with us through the hard path. Our situations may not be good, but God's character is always good and faithful, and that will never change.

Pain and suffering cloud our perception and often tempt us in our in-between times to believe God is silent or, worse yet, that God is absent and has turned his back on us when we need him most. Our cries may sound a bit like David's:

> Save me, O God,
>   for the waters have come up to my neck.
> I sink in the miry depths,
>   where there is no foothold.
> I have come into the deep waters;
>   the floods engulf me.
> I am worn out calling for help;
>   my throat is parched.
> My eyes fail,
>   looking for my God. (Ps. 69:1–3)

And yet, once we've healed from the pain and we have the scar to show for our time of woundedness, it is then that we can look in life's rearview mirror with perspective and see God's goodness, faithfulness, and redemption of our suffering.

Waiting for this perspective and walking through your circumstance with nothing in hand but faith is a challenge because pain is immediate, clouding our view of the future, and a lack of resolution causes us to despair. Many times, I've wanted God to answer my prayers in a certain way and within a specific time frame, but ultimately, God's provision was not per my agenda or my timeline, nor was it wrapped up in a neat, pretty bow.

Have you ever been—or are you perhaps currently—in God's waiting room? You prayed for an answer. Silence. You prayed for God to move. Stillness. You prayed for God to open doors and make a way. Dead end. Waiting—it's not easy. God *is* faithful, we know this to be true. But why? Why does God sometimes choose to delay? Why do we have to wait? Could it be that in waiting on God we discover if *we* are faithful? Will *we* wait? Until the answer comes, until God moves, until the door opens? Will *we* persevere in prayer and persevere in believing God even when we can't see his hand at work? Maybe God is waiting to see what *we* will do. "I wait for the LORD, my whole being waits, and in his word I put my hope" (Ps. 130:5).

Jesus's prayers in the garden of Gethsemane came from a place of deep pain. And yet he waited on God. He shared with God his desires but ultimately surrendered to God's will over his own. "Father, if you are willing, please take this cup of suffering away from me. Yet I want your will to be done, not mine" (Luke 22:42 NLT). Do we prize the healing or the Healer more? Healing is often our goal because we desire for pain to cease, but ultimately, knowing the Healer has greater benefit. In the certainty of God's goodness and faithfulness, we can walk the in-between and trust him to see us through it. We walk forward in faith, in the waiting, knowing that because God is good and faithful, even when our circumstances are not, "surely goodness and mercy shall follow me all the days of my life" (Ps. 23:6 KJV).

A Scarred Perspective

May God himself, the God of peace, sanctify you through and through. May your whole spirit, soul and body be kept blameless at the coming of our Lord Jesus Christ. The one who calls you is faithful, and he will do it. (1 Thess. 5:23–24)

𓆰 My Prayer for You 𓆰

Father, in a world where evil abounds, help this dear one to recognize your goodness and your faithfulness. Assure them of your steady hand. When things don't make sense and it seems answers are coming too slowly, assure them that they are securely held in the palm of your hand. When the ashes of their past seem too great, let them recognize the beauty that you craft from our most painful experiences when we will entrust them into your care. You are the God who loves, who cares, and who redeems all things for our good and your glory. In Jesus's name, amen.

𓆰 Recommended Playlist 𓆰

"Faithful Still," KingsPorch, © 2023 by BEC Recordings

"Changes Everything," KingsPorch, © 2023 by BEC Recordings

"Goodness of God," CeCe Winans, © 2021 by Pure Springs Gospel, Inc.

"How Good Is He," New Life Worship, © 2022 by New Life Worship

"Still God, Still Good," Here Be Lions, © 2021 by Integrity Music

SEVEN

We Are Stronger Than Whatever Tried to Hurt Us

Then the man said, "Your name will no longer be Jacob, but Israel, because you have struggled with God and with humans and have overcome."

Genesis 32:28

Because scars represent healed wounds, they also represent that we are stronger than whatever tried to hurt us. Whether our painful past includes a divorce, family conflict, life-threatening illness, violent crime, or something else, pain wants us to believe we can't go on. And in our own strength we can't. But when we're trusting in God to walk with us and strengthen us through it, we can not only survive but thrive despite the pain. Here's an example from my own life:

Born prematurely at a time when babies weighing less than three pounds rarely survived, especially without devastating physical or cognitive impairment, I spent my first days and weeks in what is now termed the NICU. Over time, I gained strength and was discharged into my parents' care.

Just a couple of days before my third birthday, however, I became seriously ill. A fever of 107 concerned doctors that brain damage would follow, if not death. My parents dutifully followed the physicians' recommendations of ice baths and alcohol rubs to attempt to reduce the fever, to no avail. Then the doctors advised giving me aspirin, not knowing I was allergic to it, which resulted in anaphylactic shock and ambulance transport to the nearest hospital. The staff worked tirelessly to pump my stomach and address the fever, never knowing the root cause of the illness that they later referred to as being *like* Reye's syndrome or *like* polio but not consistent with either. The next couple of days were touch and go, and doctors warned my parents that death was likely, and if not death, then certainly mental and physical incapacitation for the rest of my uncertain life.

Once my condition stabilized, doctors then prepared my parents for the likelihood that I might never walk again and that I would live with severe physical deformity. My mother was a strong New Zealander with a typical English resolve and essentially declared, "Not my daughter!" She determined to procure any necessary treatment to give me the greatest chance of walking again but could do nothing about the severe deformity that caused one of my legs to be almost two-inches shorter than the other—a "peg leg" incapable of developing any muscle in the calf—and a foot that to this day resembles the bound feet of Chinese girls from centuries ago and is now half the size of my other, normally formed foot. I endured years of physical therapy, and I entered elementary school wearing a leg brace, unable to participate in physical education classes or athletic pursuits. The teasing and bullying were merciless. And yet my family and I were grateful I was alive!

I didn't love the deformity that made me different from my peers, or the physical scars that marked my legs, but both attested to the fact that God spared my life after my premature birth and my illness three years later. God's prognosis was much different from the doctors'. Despite doctors' warnings that I would be mentally incapacitated the rest of my life, God saw to it that I would eventually become a wife, mother, doctor, author, speaker, and podcast host and would help others. When physicians declared that I would never walk again, God not only protected me but made me capable of routinely walking three to six miles daily, despite the pain in every step. As a child, I never realized I was different from my able-bodied peers until the enemy used their taunts and jeers to inflict shame and emotional wounds on top of the obvious physical ones I learned to hide from the world. But in hindsight, my leg-length difference, my resulting limp, my deformed leg and foot, and the physical scars from too many surgeries to count attest to the fact that the God in me is stronger than what tried to hurt me.

Crying on the Closet Floor

Jesus warned us that in this life we would experience trials. He offers no one immunity from pain and suffering; however, he has already overcome such difficulties *for us*. Remember his promise: "I have told you these things, so that in me you may have peace. In this world you will have trouble. But take heart! I have overcome the world" (John 16:33). What if, instead of viewing our scars as an ugly reminder of the heartache of this world, we appreciated them as a reflection that because of Jesus we are stronger than whatever tried to hurt us?

Have you ever wrestled with God? Have you taken to him the hurts, concerns, questions, and injustices that haven't made sense to your limited understanding? Have you ever stood firm, determining not to let go of God until he answered your prayers?

Throughout my childhood and most of my young adult years, I was raised with more than a reverence for God—more like a fear of his wrath. Job's story drew me in, and I pondered his life and his relationship with God, especially when life's hard knocks seemed to fall on him in rapid succession. Job took his licks for quite some time before coming to the end of his resolve and essentially asking God why he would allow such calamity to befall one of his servants. As a teen girl and young adult, I interpreted God's response to Job's questioning as his chastisement for Job's willingness to rage against the God of the universe. I stuffed my questions, fears, and disappointments to remain in the safety zone with God. I never questioned, never begged for answers, and had no assumption that I deserved better.

> **What if, instead of viewing our scars as an ugly reminder of the heartache of this world, we appreciated them as a reflection that because of Jesus we are stronger than whatever tried to hurt us?**

After several years of drowning in a tsunami of painful health-related circumstances, I was assured by doctors of answers and cures that never came. The disappointment burned my heart dark as charcoal ash. My hope dissolved, and I fell into a puddle of murky tears, begging God for rescue and appealing to his compassion and comfort. I was longing for a Hallmark ending to my heartache.

There was no perfectly wrapped resolution for my pain and disappointment. As I sobbed on my closet floor, trying to will God into taking my pain away, I pleaded for him to come to my rescue. To make things right. To answer my cry. No resolution came, but in that exchange, I sensed God gently chuckling, as if to say, "At least you're talking to me now. Now we can get somewhere. I've just been waiting for you to be willing to take my hand and walk this out together." My situation hadn't changed, but my perspective had, and I realized a fresh experience of peace.

Wrestling with God

Jacob's story in Genesis 25–35 endears me to this biblical great, in part because of his repeated struggle with his sin nature, which reminds me of my daily struggle to die to self. He became desperate enough to change his life that he risked wrestling with God and was then marked in a way that would forever remind him of his encounter, walking the rest of his earthly life with a limp, as I do. His life and decisions reflected repeated drama, discord, and pain—the experiences from which sacred scars are made. Conflict and crises seemed to follow Jacob, and yet he's deemed an Old Testament hero. His roller-coaster life, from poor decision-making to spiritual victories, underscores God's great work through the lives of his imperfect children.

In the biblical account of Jacob, we learn of the ramifications of pride, jealousy, and greed. Jacob was born holding on to the heel of his twin brother, Esau, and from that received his name, which means "supplanter." This name defined Jacob's early adult experience when he swindled his older brother out of his birthright, then conspired with his mother to deceive his father into giving Jacob the blessing that would have otherwise gone to his brother.

Esau threatened to kill Jacob once he learned of this treachery, and Jacob fled. He lived with and worked for his uncle Laban for twenty years, where he married, raised a family, and grew wealthy. The two men suffered a rocky relationship, both at times seeking advantage over the other. Jacob left Laban abruptly and quickly, without a proper farewell, which resulted in hot pursuit by his uncle and the threat of violence. Following the resolution of that event, Jacob turned his thoughts back to his brother, whom he messaged soliciting a meeting. The response came back that his brother was traveling to meet him with four hundred men. The day before their meeting, Jacob sent his possessions and family across the river, separating himself and Esau's men, and spent a solitary night. It was at this point in his distress about Esau's possible revenge that Jacob articulated his dependence on God, stating, "I am unworthy of all the kindness and faithfulness you have shown your servant. I had only my staff when I crossed this Jordan, but now I have become two camps" (Gen. 32:10). This God who had shown up multiple times in Jacob's fretful life but whom Jacob had seemingly relegated to the margin showed up that night. Genesis 32:24 records that "Jacob was left alone, and a man wrestled with him till daybreak." At daybreak, Jacob refused to release his opponent and demanded a blessing, realizing with whom he contended. Jacob had come face-to-face with God. God changed Jacob's name to Israel, recognizing and highlighting a change in Jacob's character. The supplanter had become "one who struggles" but was also recognized by God as one who overcame (see v. 28).

This man who had deceived and cheated, bent relationships to his advantage, and fled when he had maximized his gain or overplayed his hand finally found a worthy opponent. The God of his fathers, whom Jacob did not recognize as the one he had prayed to that night (see Gen. 32:9–12), put Jacob's hip out of place, forcing him to limp (see v. 25). This physical scar, which mirrored Jacob's relational scars, marked Jacob's "overcoming," not in the sense that he overcame God but in that he recognized God for who he was—sovereign, just, righteous, and still merciful and gracious enough to pursue relationship with a hustler like Jacob. This revelation by God himself radically realigned Jacob's view of himself, his world, and the people around him.

His reunion with Esau was almost comical in the way Jacob's gifts to his brother were offered, declined, insisted on, then accepted (see Gen. 33:8–11). Jacob described seeing Esau again as "seeing the face of God" (v. 10), an incredible statement from someone who just hours before *had* seen the face of God. Jacob went on to recognize God's graciousness to him and voiced sufficiency for what he had. Jacob valued relationship, acted and spoke humbly, recognized his dependence on God, and recognized God's abundant provision for him and his family. Was this the same man as the one who had cheated his brother, deceived his father, and almost came to blows with his uncle?

In considering the significance of Jacob's encounter with God, we can understand our own struggles through a new lens. Through our painful trials and in the struggles, God offers us strength, courage, freedom, and the ability to persevere *with* him as our Defender, our Refuge, and our Comforter. No encounter with God will leave us unchanged. God's dislocating Jacob's hip deterred his ability to escape and forced him to face his past in order to heal, move on from it, and learn that we are weak in our flesh and must depend on God's mercy and grace. For the rest of his life, when Jacob was tempted to flee, he would be reminded of his encounter with God. Rather than running away, God wants us to run *to* him.

Jacob's life attests to the hope we have that God continues to use imperfect people whose lives reflect one mistake after another and that God wants to use us, even after we spiritually stumble time and time again. We know right from wrong, and yet we still veer off the narrow path. Jacob was forced to confront his failures as he wrestled with God, for there was no other path toward rescue, just as we must acknowledge our sins, our mistakes, and our errored ways to receive God's life-changing experience of forgiveness and redemption. Some of our greatest growth opportunities come after the wrestle with pain and suffering. As we struggle with God, we come face-to-face with his character, his relentless pursuit of us, yet his gentleness in catching us.

Sometimes God must slow us down to teach us what is best. God repeatedly calls us to trust him, yet sometimes the only way we learn the importance of putting our complete trust in God is for him to allow us to walk through painful trials where we have no other hope. Is it possible that Jacob's wrestling with God wasn't so much about fighting against God but rather about fighting against his own past, pain, shame, and guilt? And is it possible that his encounter with God was less about God subduing him and more about God blessing him far beyond any blessing he'd gained through manipulative means from his father, his brother, or his uncle?

Some of our greatest growth opportunities come after the wrestle with pain and suffering.

Jacob's scars reveal that our sin, pain, and shame don't determine our identity. Scripture records that God changed Jacob's name: "Then the man said, 'Your name will no longer be Jacob, but Israel, because you have struggled with God and with humans and have overcome'" (Gen. 32:28). In Scripture, every time God bestows a new name on an individual, it marks a change in their character as it is renewed by God. Jacob's new name, Israel, represented his struggle with God and reflected his lifelong struggle with those around him, with his sin, and with the God who could save him. Jacob had previously been very independent and had acted upon his impulses to ensure that he got what he both wanted and felt was due him, and yet Jacob's limp was transformative because it signified his dependence on God going forward.

In their wrestling, where Jacob earned a permanent limp, God spared his life and taught Jacob more about himself. Just as in the case of Jacob's limp, our scars are a reminder that the God in us is stronger than anything that tries to come against and overpower us. Rather than being an evil dictator, God gives us free will. He's not looking for a slave/master relationship. Ultimately, he desires relationship and righteousness, and he will use whatever means are necessary to teach us about him—even our pain, including pain from our own poor decisions and natural consequences from our mistakes.

Jacob wrestled with God until God blessed him. Jacob had already received his earthly father's blessing, but he'd gained it through control and manipulation, when the only blessing that would truly satisfy was the Lord's. How often do we strive in our own strength to make things happen, only to find the results unfulfilling and demanding our continued attention and effort. In contrast, and like Jacob, we have the opportunity to learn that surrendering to God's will and God's way is far superior. Jacob tended to exhibit pride, arrogance, and greed, yet his resulting scar in the form of a physical limp may have been the means God used to teach him about humility and that nothing else would satisfy more than personal dependence on the God of sufficiency.

We are often unaware of our unconscious dependence on our own strength and effort until we are put in a situation that requires us to go beyond what we would normally believe ourselves capable of. On the other side of pain, we realize that God's strength in us is greater than whatever tried to hurt us.

A Scarred Perspective

He gives strength to the weary
    and increases the power of the weak.
Even youths grow tired and weary,
    and young men stumble and fall;
but those who hope in the LORD
    will renew their strength.

They will soar on wings like eagles;
>they will run and not grow weary,
>they will walk and not be faint. (Isa. 40:29–31)

My Prayer for You

Father, we confess we've become so accustomed to believing the lie that "if it's going to be, it's up to me." Help this dear one to recognize that all good things, including the healing of our pain and suffering, come from you. Thank you that you are greater than anything that rises up against us and causes us heartache. We know that Jesus defeated pain, infirmity, sin, and death on the cross, as evidenced by the scars he bore after his resurrection. Help us to honor our scars since they provide a visible testimony that because of you in us, we are stronger than whatever tried to rise up against us. In Jesus's name, amen.

Recommended Playlist

"The God Who Fights for Me," ZOE Music, © 2020 by ZOE LA/Watershed Music Group

"Same God," Elevation Worship, © 2022 by Elevation Worship Records

"Champion," Bethel Music, © 2020 by Bethel Music

"That Was Then, This Is Now," Josh Wilson, © 2015 by Sparrow Records

"Say I Won't," MercyMe, © 2021 by MercyMe

EIGHT

We Are Overcomers

You, dear children, are from God and have overcome them, because the one who is in you is greater than the one who is in the world.

1 John 4:4

Overcoming may look different to each of us. For some, overcoming is the eradication of pain. Sometimes it means righting a wrong. For others, it means pushing through to complete something against the odds.

For my friends Bill and Pam Farrel, their sacred scars attest to their overcoming generational dysfunction in marriage. They determined not to repeat the relationship patterns modeled for them and to change the trajectory for their marriage, putting God and his principles first. Here's their overcoming story:

———————■———————

My husband and I come from such dysfunctional homes that friends comment on what a miracle our forty-three-year marriage is.

I am the firstborn daughter of an alcoholic, often suicidal father whose verbal abuse and rage issues occasionally escalated into violence. My dad's father was the town drunk, and his ability to stay employed varied from year to year. My dad's mother was a one-room schoolhouse teacher and struggled to provide for her large brood. She was a God-fearing woman, but life's responsibilities were heavy, so many of her children, especially her sons, followed in their dad's footsteps with addictions to drinking and smoking. Most of these sons' marriages ended in divorce.

My mother was born into the home of a farmer and shepherd, but her parents and their large extended family who had immigrated from New Zealand were members of a cult. My maternal grandparents had a solid and loving marriage, but the spiritual atmosphere was confusing. My parents married young and almost immediately bore me. Dad's drinking escalated, so Mom frequently placed me on her hip and walked to the little town's bar to drag my drunk dad home.

After my sister and brother were born, my mom's best friend, witnessing the family chaos, invited us to church. Mom was desperate for change, so she dressed us in the nicest clothes we owned and ushered us into the tiny church with a tiny steeple in a tiny town. Even as a seven-year-old, I knew I had met people of love, so I knew I wanted to know the Author of love, Jesus. We sang songs of God's love, I memorized Bible verses, and I was encouraged to pick a toy out of a treasure chest: a little white cross that glowed in the dark and had printing that read, "Jesus Lives."

One night, my dad raged after drinking all day and night. My mom tried to calm him, but the shouting grew louder and I feared for my siblings. I gathered them into my room, tucked them into my bed, and pushed the chest of drawers in front of the door so Dad couldn't get in and hurt us. I shut off the light, crawled in bed, and huddled up with them. Glowing in the dark was that little cross, shining out hope. I prayed, "Lord, the pastor told us you are stronger than anything, more powerful than anyone—you even rose from the dead. Please come into my life and be my best friend, Savior, and Lord. And PS, God, if you would work it out, I would really love to marry a pastor one day."

Meanwhile, just miles from the debauchery of Hollywood, a cute curly-haired little boy lived on a tightrope, trying to navigate his life between a genius rocket-engineer father and a mother struggling with mental illness, anger, paranoia, and depression. As youngsters, Bill and his brother were given a few quarters on Sundays and instructed to walk to the neighborhood church. This little church gave Bill a Bible that had a cover depicting Jesus with children.

Bill and his brother lived in a house that was beautiful on the outside but full of chaos and conflict on the inside. Weeks passed without them seeing their depressed mother, who was isolated in bed. To survive, their dad gave them money to walk to the store to buy groceries and cook for themselves. By age eight, Bill had self-taught culinary skills, did his own laundry, and had learned to hide from his mom's volatile anger when she intermittently emerged. By high school, he avoided home by participating in athletics. A friend on his basketball team had a dad who was a pastor, but surprisingly, Bill's vivid spiritual awakening occurred when he snuck out of the house to see the movie *The Exorcist* with another friend. Bill likes to say, "I was scared to life!" For weeks, Bill couldn't sleep, terrorized by thoughts of the devil and his evil powers.

One night, Bill picked up his childhood Bible and read 1 John 4:4: "Greater is he that is in you, than he that is in the world" (KJV). He prayed and asked Christ into his life, and for the first time in weeks, Bill slept soundly all night! Within a few weeks, Bill's mother banned him and his brother from attending church, so they started a student-led Bible study that grew to over sixty high schoolers.

My family moved to California, and Mom, my siblings, and I began attending a Bible-teaching church. I was invited to a Campus Crusade for Christ (Cru) event as a college freshman, and one of the leaders challenged me to attend a discipleship Bible study. She mentored me in ways to deepen my faith: Bible study, daily devotions, prayer, sharing my faith, and obeying God.

When Bill entered college, he and his brother also attended Cru Bible studies. Our paths crossed, and one day Bill asked, "What did God teach you today?" I was delighted that this tan, handsome, and *godly* guy was talking to me! Our relationship deepened and Bill proposed.

A few months later, we wed in the local church where we eventually served on staff. (God had answered my prayer and led Bill to become a pastor!) We were blessed with godly mentors who taught us how to avoid the unhealthy relationship patterns we'd observed in our parents and grandparents. Our hearts have remained bonded through sharing God's Word, serving Jesus, and pouring out the truths of how to love like God with our family and friends. We have three grown and married sons and seven grandchildren being raised in the faith. Through the power of God, we saw the Lord break the chains of sin, dysfunction, and destructive family patterns that were present in our heritages and allow us to live as overcomers.

Our genetic and spiritual lineages impact our lives, sometimes leaving wounds so deep only God can diagnose and treat them. We determined to help other married couples "love wise" and avoid the marital and personal dysfunction we witnessed by writing, speaking, teaching, and offering resources through our biblically based marriage ministry, LoveWise.com. We find significance in this passage from Colossians:

> [Give] joyful thanks to the Father, who has qualified you to share in the inheritance of his holy people in the kingdom of light. For he has rescued us from the dominion of darkness and brought us into the kingdom of the Son he loves, in whom we have redemption, the forgiveness of sins. (Col. 1:12–14)

What Does Overcoming Look Like?

The implicit ideal within our culture seems to be a life without pain. Perhaps overcoming isn't living a pain-free existence but putting one foot in front of the other when everything within you begs you to quit. I wonder if Jesus ever felt like this. Jesus is our model Overcomer. Jesus knew his mission, and part of that was the same as ours today: to point others to a saving relationship with God. He bridged heaven and earth on our behalf. And yet he also experienced physical, emotional, relational, and spiritual pain along his ministry path. His own townspeople and brothers rejected him. Even though his disciples witnessed his greatest miracles, they didn't understand much of what he preached and rebuked him when he told them of his imminent death. His disciples couldn't stay awake with him in his moment of greatest need, and one not only rejected him but betrayed him. Jesus suffered in the most unimaginable ways, but through that he can relate to our suffering. "For we do not have a high priest who is unable to empathize with our weaknesses" (Heb. 4:15). He understands. He empathizes. He hurts with us and for us. He also knows there is always a greater purpose in our suffering, just as there was in his.

In my painful circumstances, as I've waited for God to bring healing to my heart and to the situation, I've been tempted to think that God has turned his back on me when I haven't sensed or felt his presence, when I haven't been able to hear his voice, when I've wondered if he was angry with me. When we are at our weakest, longing for rescue and comfort, we are most susceptible to the enemy's lies. My pain has traditionally been the worst in the evening hours and into the ebony-dark night . . . the time when my thoughts are less preoccupied with my daily to-dos and free to roam and fret. The enemy's lies are deafening then. *If God loved you, he would have healed you by now. Your sins are a disgrace to the*

> **Perhaps overcoming isn't living a pain-free existence but putting one foot in front of the other when everything within you begs you to quit.**

God you claim to serve—why would he choose to forgive you? You long to feel God's presence, but he has abandoned you in your pain and suffering.

In the darkest moment recorded in history, Jesus wrestled with God. In the garden he prayed that the cup of his suffering, crucifixion, and death would be taken from him yet added that he was in deference to his Father's will (see Matt. 26:39). From the cross he pleaded the words from Psalm 22:1, "My God, my God, why have you forsaken me?" Jesus did not want to go through a painful, torturous death, and yet he recognized his Father's greater work within that hour of his suffering. Even as Jesus despaired, he yielded to God's will in the moment and continued to wait on God's deliverance. Jesus allowed himself to be dependent on God, even as God permitted his death and even as he unfairly carried the weight of the world's sin on the cross. Jesus bent low, wept, and bled on our behalf. What Jesus accomplished on the cross we could never do for ourselves. Through his death and resurrection, he showed us in patience and faith what overcoming looks like, both the depths from which it rises and the quiet triumph it brings forth.

The scars in Christ's hands and feet proved to those he appeared to in resurrected form that he was who he said he was, he had done what he said he would do, and in overcoming sin, disease, and death for our sakes, he was stronger than that which tried to kill him.

Sometimes overcoming doesn't look like conquering. Sometimes overcoming looks like keeping our focus on God instead of on our painful situation. In my deepest pain, when hopelessness threatened to cut my last strand of resolve, I cried out to God, "I can't do this if you don't intervene. I have nothing left to give. My heart and my soul despair for your touch. Don't turn your back on me." We often look at healing as a one-and-done scenario, but I suspect God looks at our healing in terms of layers and depths. The lame man Jesus encountered at the pool of Bethesda received his physical healing, but that was just the first part of his path to living as a new, healed man. The lessons of his scars serve as encouragement to us today.

I'm Healed, Now What?

The pool of Bethesda in Jerusalem was recognized as a place of miraculous healing for those with infirmities ranging from paralysis to blindness. Imagine, if you will, struggling to do anything for yourself for almost four decades because a birth defect, illness, or injury left you an invalid, too sick or weak to care for your own basic needs. In such a state, you're dependent on others to feed you, to clothe you, to take you places, and to provide for your financial needs. It is a lonely existence when you feel you are a burden on others but have no other options.

When I read this man's story, the longing in his heart and the aching in his soul are palpable, as are the likely human emotions that accompany his existence: frustration, blame, and helplessness, if not hopelessness. How much longer would he have to live at the mercy of others and wait for a rare moment of miracle from the healing waters? His skin was surely taut from the harmful effects of the sun's reflection from the pool; his muscles were undoubtedly atrophied from decades of underuse. People likely ignored or scoffed at him as they passed by, selfishly seeking their own healing over his. His esteem was almost certainly as fragile as his body. In a very brief encounter with Jesus, though, his entire life changed.

The narrative reads like this:

> When Jesus saw him lying there and learned that he had been in this condition for a long time, he asked him, "Do you want to get well?"

"Sir," the invalid replied, "I have no one to help me into the pool when the water is stirred. While I am trying to get in, someone else goes down ahead of me."

Then Jesus said to him, "Get up! Pick up your mat and walk." At once the man was cured; he picked up his mat and walked. (John 5:6–9)

Before his healing, I wonder if in his mind the crippled man believed God was done with him and that his life was worthless. But God wasn't done writing his story, and he's not done with yours either. While I believe that God didn't create us for infirmity or pain, and that he weeps when we weep, ultimately God is more concerned with our relationship with him and our eternal destiny than he is with our comfort. If healing us will draw us closer in relationship to him, as it did with the invalid, God will use whatever means are necessary to accomplish that. We can't know for sure, but I wonder if, once the lame man received his healing and life changed so dramatically for him, the joy he felt diminished his memory of the pain.

Perhaps the greatest of many lessons from the scars of this man's experience as a lifelong invalid healed by an ephemeral encounter with the Savior and Healer of the world is his becoming an overcomer. In an unbelievable act of compliance, this lame man pulled his legs up under himself and stood, an impossible act not just from his infirmity but doubly so from the atrophy and loss of coordination that accompanied it and from his state of mind as an invalid.

So many of us need healing, yet we're too afraid to jump into the deep end of a relationship with God. Our human tendency is often to stay in our areas of known discomfort rather than risk the discomfort of the unknown. In our pain, we often default to excuses to assuage our conscience—"I have no one to help me into the pool when the water is stirred. While I am trying to get in, someone else goes down ahead of me" (John 5:7)—but our excuses don't hold weight with God. God is looking for obedience, not excuses.

You see, even in literally stepping into his miraculous healing, this man suddenly had to deal with a drastic change to his identity. Instead of decades of being "the lame man," he was now "the healed man," which came with some notoriety. He had to find gainful employment, and his social circle changed. Scary things!

When we are suffering and in pain, waiting on God to heal our physical bodies, our hearts, our relationships, we often grow weary in the waiting and jealous of what we see God doing in the lives of others. Sometimes we become so consumed with comparing our situation, our painful wilderness, and our want of healing with others' that we effectively take our eyes off God, no longer pursuing a deeper relationship with him. I wonder if the invalid in this story did that too: Every day as he waited by the edge of the pool, did he grow jealous of those who entered the pool infirm and in pain only to walk out healed and whole, leaving that terrible chapter of their lives behind them while he lay there wanting? Perhaps this lame man adopted a mantle of hopelessness after all those years of waiting to be healed. Often, we try everything in our power to fix our situation or heal our pain before we fall flat on our backs with no other place to look but up to the God of heaven.

There was a crowd of people at Bethesda, but as far as we know, the lame man was the only one Jesus healed that day. That serves as a lesson for us. This man's experience illustrates that when God intends to do a work in us, he will seek us out, find us, and do as he plans. Jesus focuses on us as individuals and what we each need in our walk with him. God never withholds that which is good from his children—it just may not look the way we expect or come when we desire. "For the Lord God is a sun and shield; the LORD bestows favor and honor; no good thing does he withhold from those whose walk is blameless" (Ps. 84:11).

Furthermore, while God can do anything without our help, he often partners with us to give us the greater blessing of working with him toward an end. Jesus first gave the lame man the command to pick up his mat and walk, and then he was instantly healed. Often, God is looking for our obedience, even when things don't make sense. Sometimes it is those circumstances that require the most faith—the one thing God values from us most of all. Yet God never asks us to do anything without giving us the strength and power to do it.

An encounter with Jesus will allow us to see things about ourselves we never believed possible. This man was lame for decades, dependent on others, unable to care for himself or work to meet his needs. But in one brief meeting, he shed his identity as the lame man. One transient, timely encounter with Jesus can take us from hurting to healed, despairing to hopeful, disbelieving to faith filled. While we may focus on our physical healing, God is also concerned about healing our hearts and our souls, creating sacred scars. "Later Jesus found him at the temple and said to him, 'See, you are well again. Stop sinning or something worse may happen to you'" (John 5:14). Furthermore, the lame man's faith was strengthened enough that he risked telling the Jews that Jesus, his Savior and Messiah, healed him. Perhaps that man's miraculous healing was an example: God invites us to share with others our sacred scars, which attest to the fact that we overcame, so that they know healing is possible.

A Scarred Perspective

No, in all these things we are more than conquerors through him who loved us. (Rom. 8:37)

My Prayer for You

Father, I come to you on behalf of this dear one who has gone through a season of pain and suffering. Thank you that in your Word, you tell us the way is through. Let them see the truth that they are truly overcomers. Thank you for the shed blood of Jesus that overcame sin, death, disease, and suffering. We look forward to an eternity in the absence of pain and suffering. In Jesus's name, amen.

Recommended Playlist

"Son of Suffering," Bethel Music, © 2021 by Bethel Music

"All Things New," Planetshakers, © 2020 by Planetshakers

"Don't You Give Up on Me," Brandon Lake, © 2022 by Tribl Records

"Overcomer," Mandisa, © 2013 by Sparrow Records

"Never Has," FOUNT, © 2023 by The Harmony Group, LLC

NINE

We Are Loved

The LORD your God is with you,
  the Mighty Warrior who saves.
He will take great delight in you;
  in his love he will no longer rebuke you,
  but will rejoice over you with singing.
                                        Zephaniah 3:17

My friend Aliene is poised, intelligent, genuine, and compassionate, which could precipitate the impression that she has had an easy life and has never wrestled with torment or despair. But, friends, we all have our areas of struggle. Aliene's early life wasn't tranquil or rudimental. She grappled early on to believe she was loved, which shaped many of her adult interactions. Many of us have wondered the same thing: *Am I worthy of love? If others don't love me, how can God, who knows my every thought, belief, and deed? If God allowed such anguish in my life, can he be trusted to love me?* In his kindness, God provided Aliene the revelation that changed her perspective and set her on a new path, and she now uses her scars to help others. I think her sacred scars will encourage you:

While God's framework for family is perfect, we are not, and under the weight of a broken world, the experiences many of us have with families are fractured rather than whole, distorted rather than ideal. This was certainly true for me. As a child, I experienced mental, emotional, and at times, physical abuse. Performance, or being good, was a way to protect myself. During middle school, a figurative bomb dropped in our family, which intensified my pain. I felt angry, confused, and abandoned. I didn't recognize it then, but my abandonment issues precipitated a constant need to secure love from others at any cost, which only yielded more brokenness.

At one point, feeling so desperate to be loved but not getting my needs met, I attempted suicide. During this period of crisis, my subconscious formed a deep, destructive drumbeat of lies leading to a rhythm of codependency to cope:

- I am not worth fighting for.
- I must work hard to succeed and thus prove I am lovable.
- I cannot allow myself to be weak or I'll get hurt again.
- I must be the best—anything less than perfect is unacceptable.
- I must please others or I will never earn their love.

Although I never acknowledged or articulated these lies, they became my false formulas to live by—inner vows I felt certain would fix my broken heart and help me find happiness, worth, identity, love, and ultimately, life. At this juncture, performance became more than a way to self-protect and gain love; it was a weapon of revenge to prove to anyone who hurt me that they were wrong about me—that I was worth fighting for and worthy of love.

Over the years, in an attempt to create the life of peace and love that I craved, my codependency coping mechanism led me to adopt unhealthy relationships and controlling tendencies. Even though I became a Christian when I was twenty-three, the well-worn patterns I'd used to cope with life remained entrenched within my approach to life. I brought my codependency and performance mentality into my relationship with God. A fixer and rescuer with a ferocious victim mentality, I never really walked under God's blessing. My codependency flew right under the radar of self-focused good works, and it increased because the messages I heard in church and how I interpreted them through the lens of my life supported my codependency drumbeat.

The enemy used lies about God, myself, and others against me, keeping this codependency going and preventing me from growing in the freedom that Christ offers. I did not understand that laying down my life for God did not mean pleasing others but instead making God my primary focus. I didn't see my codependency for what it was: idolatry of humankind. I didn't recognize that if I had to perform to earn love, it wasn't love at all.

Waving my victim flag kept me self-focused. God was not my source of love because the world's false definition of love ruled my heart, and I ran headlong in pursuit. I confused forgiving others with trusting, and I failed to set boundaries with unhealthy people. Self-reliant moral striving sabotaged God's work in me and wore me out. Hustling hard for inner healing felt like an endless, frustrating chase. Busyness prevented me from being fully present with my family. I was born again but burnt out and sucked dry because I pursued people as the source for value and love.

Like the Samaritan woman at the well, I was trapped by those lies in the never-ending cycle of searching for that something, or someone, to satisfy the ache in my soul and fill the universal desire to love and be loved. But the truth remained: unless I connected to the Healer through complete, daily God-dependency, my search for healing was futile.

One day, the enemy created what I now consider the perfect storm. Through my choice to become enmeshed in an unhealthy friendship and attempt to find my worth through ministry efforts, the perfect life I had worked so hard to erect came crashing down like a house built on sand at high tide. But in the rubble of failure, an epic new journey began—an awareness and unraveling of codependency through God's beautiful refining fire, which would open my arms to authentic intimacy with Jesus, freedom through God-dependency, and living in the power of the Holy Spirit by putting God first.

Now my heart beats with a new daily rhythm that rests and relies on God's Word and power. And I do this one day at a time, one step at a time, walking by faith in God's living Word in daily dependence on him. I traded my pursuit of perfection to pursue an intimate friendship with Jesus and love for and from the Father. I am free to put God first and experience the fruit that flows from abiding in him—including loving others with God's authentic love. And this love spilled over into my family of four, where I experienced and gave true biblical, unconditional love for the first time. God healed my fractured heart and transformed my pain into parchment paper, where he wrote his story of redemption and illustrated the power of God-dependency through my new life of freedom.

God's restoration story did not end there; he gave me a passion for helping other women rise out of past trauma to live treasured, knowing they are valued, cherished, and loved by God not for what they do, which could never be enough, but because of whose they are—his.

A Holy Whisper

Until our battle wounds are healed, we run the risk of them resurfacing, like when a scab is ripped off a skinned knee. When healing comes and scars emerge, the pain no longer exists, despite the memories of a painful past. And the lessons we learn along the journey inform who we are going forward.

Following the death of my father when I was a young teen, my tender heart embraced the lie that I was an abandoned, fatherless daughter. My father was the youngest of five children, yet the first of his siblings to die, by several decades. Many people would offhandedly say, "I don't know how I'll make it when one of my parents dies," and each time I heard it, a bit of my heart hardened because the pain of living life without my father left an unfulfilled longing and ache deep within me. Every time I bumped up against the truth that my father was no longer a part of my life and wouldn't see any of my major milestones, scabs were ripped off, leaving my wounds bare and throbbing again.

> When healing comes and scars emerge, the pain no longer exists, despite the memories of a painful past. And the lessons we learn along the journey inform who we are going forward.

I knew my dad loved me, but with him gone, who would love me now? In my late teens and early adulthood, I numbed the pain by staying busy. It helped only until the house was quiet or I lay in bed, finally still for the day. I neglected to attend school father-daughter events—it was too much like adding salt to a wound. When I graduated from high school, I looked up into the stands to see my brother, mother, and stepfather, but one of the most important people in my life was missing, and that diminished my joy. My father wasn't alive to give my husband his blessing or my hand in marriage or to walk me down the aisle when we got married, and I felt cheated. Every year when the anniversary of my father's death approaches, my thoughts turn to what could have been, should have been. It still grieves me that neither of my children got to know either of my parents.

I'll probably never know this side of heaven why God allows such early deaths of some of his most committed servants. My dad loved the Lord with his whole heart, and he loved others well, including me. He had a fun sense of humor, and everyone felt seen and loved by him. I was fortunate because he offered me a strong spiritual legacy. I still miss my dad: his hugs, his laughter, his wisdom, his compassion, but mostly his love. I can only hope he'd be proud of the woman I've become.

About a decade ago, another anniversary of my father's death passed, and I numbed the pain by working hard, justifying it by thinking, *It was my dad who instilled such a strong work ethic within me.* The problem was, working to anesthetize the pain didn't heal the barbed-wire sorrow embedded in my heart. Believing I'd been abandoned and orphaned by my earthly father, I increasingly withdrew from my heavenly Father, unconsciously fearing that he, too, would desert me. I longed for my father to be proud of his daughter. I craved his love, validation, and acceptance. But since I couldn't receive it from him this side of heaven and feared the fallout if I didn't receive it from my heavenly Father, I sought it from people and performance. I studied hard and pursued my board certification in neuropsychology. The pressure to perform well was immense, and as the stress mounted, I crumbled. I lay on the bed in the hotel room I had rented to study without distraction, sobbing and feeling like a failure, not feeling up to the challenge I'd voluntarily pursued. I had never heard the audible voice of God, but at that moment I experienced what I can only describe as a holy whisper to my heart. It was as if God's Holy Spirit physically inhabited the room with me, cloaked me in a blanket of loving-kindness, and whispered truth that set my performance-driven heart free: *You're already successful in my eyes. No accomplishment means more to me than the fact that I've adopted you as my daughter and you, in turn, have put your trust in me. You no longer live abandoned or orphaned but fully and completely loved and accepted by me, not for what you do but because of whose you are.* Friend, isn't that what we all truly crave? Unconditional love, despite our pain and our shame. And it's already ours for the taking.

Is It Really Love If You Have to Earn It?

Life brings about plenty of opportunities to experience pain in its various permutations. It's virtually impossible to escape this life unscathed by the hurtful words and actions of others, which contribute to relationship pain. The casual comments and opinions of others regarding why we've endured hardship bring secondary pain: how our diet has "caused" the cancer we've been diagnosed with, how our imperfect parenting "led to" having a prodigal child, how our aging body "led to" a spouse's wandering eye, and so on. Another form of secondary pain results from others expressing their certainty of what we "should" do to right our situation: that perfect pill or potion they are certain will cure our medical diagnosis, the prescribed acts of service that are sure to persuade God to release our child from prison, the specifically worded prayer that will turn our spouse's heart toward home. These expressions are, at the least, guilt-inducing and shame-promoting but also proud and arrogant beyond that. While there are many problems with attitudes and comments like these, the overarching result is that it takes our attention off the One who can right our wrongs, heal our hurts, and redeem what was lost and refocuses us on what *we* could've done or should do.

Aliene discussed the pain she endured secondary to her co-dependency tendencies to find love. Relationship pain, loss, and grief often contribute to us doing "whatever it takes" to try to secure favorable opinions, fond affection, and the devotion of others. Whenever we focus on making others happy rather than first following hard after what delights God's heart, it sets up a dangerous potential for idolizing the opinions of people. Friend, those will never permanently satisfy. They only encourage our heart until the next demand is made. When we focus on pleasing others at the risk of our authentic self, it's like showing others a bouquet of roses, hoping to cover up the weeds in our garden. Inauthenticity breeds discontentment and will never satisfy the longing in our hearts to be loved; only Jesus can do that.

Unfortunately, the melody of love that God sings over us each day gets drowned out by the screams of our pain, the voice of culture, the shouts of our task lists, and the whispers of the enemy. If you don't hear anything else between the pages of this book, please hear this: You are already loved by God, and nothing you've done nor anything that happens to you will change that. You do not fight this alone. "The LORD your God is with you, the Mighty Warrior who saves. He will take great delight in you; in his love he will no longer rebuke you, but will rejoice over you with singing" (Zeph. 3:17). Let his love envelop you and bring peace to your pain-filled heart and purpose to your sacred scars. Because he loves you, he will not waste your heartache.

Human tendency is to judge things, people, and circumstances, but our judgment is usually biased by our predetermined rubric for what is right versus wrong, good versus bad, successful versus unsuccessful, perfect versus marred, or memorable versus forgettable. Even with a God-given discerning spirit, we can't fully know the heart of another, so we tend to judge by outward appearances. God warned about this. "The LORD does not look at the things people look at. People look at the outward appearance, but the LORD looks at the heart" (1 Sam. 16:7). Isn't it amazing to think that God looks at our heart, sees all the pain, hurt, anger, malice, resentment, jealousy, pride, and every other part of us that we would be loath for others to see, and *yet* he still offers us unconditional love? "For I am convinced that neither death nor life, neither angels nor demons, neither the present nor the future, nor any powers, neither height nor depth, nor anything else in all creation, will be able to separate us from the love of God that is in Christ Jesus our Lord" (Rom. 8:38–39).

Looking for Love in All the Wrong Places

Codependency wasn't a label in biblical times, but there is a story in John 4 that reflects a tendency to move from person to person trying to gain love, only to learn that it is already freely given from the One who matters. The story takes place around a well. In his travels, Jesus stopped at the well midday and asked a Samaritan woman there for a drink of water. This encounter surprised her because Jewish men didn't usually associate with Samaritans and because she was accustomed to being shunned by her community. But God never does anything randomly, without significance or purpose, and the same is true when Scripture says, "Now he *had* to go through Samaria" (John 4:4, emphasis added). Jesus did everything with purpose, so we might suspect he *had* to go to Samaria to specifically change this woman's life in an unexpected encounter at the well. Jesus saw the unseen, shared a meal with the unclean, and visited with the rejected—he was the embodiment of perfect love.

This Samaritan woman had lived her life repeatedly trying to find love, only to be used and discarded. She knew the pain of being deemed not good enough by others, used for their gain, then tossed aside when she no longer met their needs. Her pain from their rejection was likely complicated by secondary pain through the comments, snickers, and jeers of others thinking themselves somehow better when their sins were not as public and well-known. The other women in her town didn't include her in their regular sojourns to fill their water jars, leaving her to walk out her shame, guilt, and regret with each step as she daily made her way to the well.

Jesus saw the unseen, shared a meal with the unclean, and visited with the rejected—he was the embodiment of perfect love.

I can imagine her surprise when, expecting judgment and criticism, she met a man there who not only spoke to her but didn't condemn her. Scripture doesn't share her intimate thoughts, but if I put myself in her sandals, I wonder if her internal dialogue went something like this: *What is he doing here when it is so hot? And why is he speaking to me? Is he culturally insensitive? My own neighbors pretend I don't exist or whisper behind my back; he must be unaware of the neighborhood gossip. Why would he think I would speak to a stranger, much less offer the only thing of value I have left to give anyone—a way to retrieve water?*

I've been in similar situations . . . maybe you have too. Not specifically with her exact areas of struggle, but with wanting to be loved, seeking it in dishonorable places and by doing inappropriate things, and then being surprised later when God planted special people in my life who extended his love, despite my many shortcomings. I've also experienced times when I anticipated rejection from others and in ways caused it to happen as a bit of a self-fulfilling prophecy, and yet God never withdrew his love; he can't—he is love. On occasion, I've worn myself thin trying to be all things to all people, coming up empty, and crying out to God to show me a touch of his love.

Jesus was alone when he encountered the woman drawing water from the well. She didn't know who Jesus was or what he could offer her, which is true for so many of us today: until we've experienced the fullness of his love, we equate Jesus to the relations we've had that have been fraught with brokenness and despair. This woman's situation was ironic in that Jesus was thirsty and asking for water from her jar, but at the same time, he had something greater to offer her: living water that provided salvation, eternal life, acceptance, and love from the One who could fully satisfy her every need (see John 4:10, 13–18). In that brief interchange, he offered his willingness to reach across societal norms, see her, acknowledge her, care about her, interact with her, and extend mercy, grace, and love, the very things her heart most needed and longed for. He quickly revealed that he already knew her more than she could have imagined, yet Jesus's tone wasn't condemning as much as it was nonchalantly factual—enough for her to recognize him as some form of prophet. There was something about this Jesus—he knew her desolation and loved her in it.

When I consider this account, I'm struck by the boldness with which Jesus dismissed the societal rules and offered tenderness to this woman who was used to living her life in isolation, wounded and under condemnation by others. She spent her adult life seeking to be loved, only to be repeatedly rebuffed, shamed, and left with the sorrow of rejection and abandonment. In a matter of moments, Jesus showed her what true love was and that she didn't have to earn it; he freely gave it.

Her shame was irradicated in a moment with One who let her share her story and held her scars as sacred. Can't you just imagine how her encounter with Jesus changed her? She returned to town excited to tell people that this man, Jesus, knew the sins of her past and yet loved her anyway. Her transformation was so great because of his love that she didn't even try to hide the sins of her past from Jesus or her townspeople. His love healed her shame and rebirthed her identity. In this brief interaction, the woman went from isolated to known, cast out to forgiven, unworthy to valued, unlovable to loved. She no longer lived beneath the shroud of her sordid past but had her sacred scars to show for it.

Her sacred scars tell a story of receiving the one thing she had always wanted but never received: validation that she was worthy of love not because of anything she did but because Jesus is love. Jesus's interaction with this woman fulfilled her deepest longing and healed her heart. But their interaction had a ripple effect, as God's healing in our lives often does: Scripture reveals that *because* of her sacred scar story of Jesus seeing her, interacting with her despite knowing all she had done in her past, and lovingly offering himself to her in the form of living water, many other Samaritans in her town began to believe in Jesus (see John 4:39). Her encounter, her interaction with a stranger, bolstered her own faith and increased the faith of many others. "They said to the woman, 'We no longer believe just because of what you said; now we have heard for ourselves, and we know that this man really is the Savior of the world'" (John 4:42). Living in the light of Jesus's love transforms us, heals our hurts, and shines as a light for others to see.

Friend, our painful past is often that which teaches us most about the nature of God. We tend to attribute human characteristics to God because our finite minds cannot grasp his infinite ways. We attribute limitations to God's mercy, grace, forgiveness, acceptance, and love based on what we've received from others. When we grasp the fact that God *knew* us before he knit us in our mother's womb (see Jer. 1:5)—he *knew* our choices, our actions, our sins before we ever committed them, he *knew* the torment we would endure, and yet he gave us his Son to bridge the gap between our painful past and God's perfect eternity—we can walk with our head held high despite our pain and despite the opinions of others.

A Scarred Perspective

And hope does not put us to shame, because God's love has been poured out into our hearts through the Holy Spirit, who has been given to us. (Rom. 5:5)

My Prayer for You

Father, I thank you that you loved us even before we were born and that our pain, suffering, brokenness, and mistakes don't change that. Help these dear ones to know the truth that nothing separates them from your everlasting love. Thank you that you love us too much to leave us where we are and that you walk with us through our pain to transformation in the form of our sacred scars. In Jesus's name, amen.

Recommended Playlist

"Steady Love," FOUNT, © 2023 by The Harmony Group, LLC

"Loved by You," Riley Clemmons, © 2023 by Capitol CMG, Inc.

"My Rest," FOUNT, © 2023 by The Harmony Group, LLC

"Fighting for My Heart," KXC and Rich & Lydia Dicas, © 2020 by KXC Music

"Found a Love," 7 Hills Worship, © 2021 by 7 Hills Church

TEN

We Are Already Accepted

However, those the Father has given me will come to me, and I will never reject them.

John 6:37 NLT

Have you ever struggled to believe you were enough? To know that you have value just because you are you? To realize that you are already accepted unconditionally by the God who created you simply because you are his? Or have you wasted moments or years trying to gain the acceptance of others, only to realize that the acceptance and approval of others are temporary and dim when your efforts to maintain them fade like the last moments of a summer sunset?

I lived many of my preadult years hearing the message from teachers, other adults, and peers that because I was flawed, I had no value, and I consequently felt rejected. Lecrae Moore writes, "If you live for people's acceptance, you'll die from their rejection."[1] The more I tried to be accepted, the more frustrated and hurt I grew by their rebuffs. When my mother became angry, I received her silent treatment, which always felt like a form of rejection. I falsely learned that perfection was required for acceptance; consequently, I concluded the same about God. Maybe you've been there.

My friend Jessica lived much of her life feeling rejected by others and, because of her wounds, rejected others. Eventually, she learned she was fully accepted by the One whose opinion matters. He healed her heart, and she learned to extend openness, acceptance, compassion, and tenderness to others. Perhaps you will find a bit of yourself in her sacred scars story:

Rejection touched my life at an early age through my parents' divorce, unsympathetic teachers, and fickle, immature peers. Despite having a few good friends throughout childhood, some wonderful teachers, and parents who loved me as best they could, rejection took root in me. Because of the painful lacerations to my heart, rejection became something for me to avoid at all costs. I strove for people's approval and tucked away each disapproval in a dark, hidden vault in my heart.

Rejection wounds festered for years, and the bandage of perfection became something I wore for protection. But perfection doesn't guarantee acceptance, and pursuing other people's approval didn't squelch my fear and anticipation of rejection. In fact, striving for perfection made my fear of rejection worse because the stakes grew higher, and I grew misshapen—I attempted to be what other people valued but lost my own value in the process.

Before God knocked on this secret hideaway, I dismissed people who rejected me and favored those who didn't. Not only did I fear rejection but I consequently rejected people too. It became a vicious cycle of fearing rejection, real and perceived; trying to be perfect to avoid others' rebuffs but experiencing them anyway; and then rejecting those who rejected me. Around my fortieth birthday, I realized that trying to rejection-proof my life wasn't helping me grow into the woman God made me to be.

Living fearfully didn't allow God's courage to flow through me. Pursuing other people's positive opinions and avoiding their negative ones made their approval of me a higher priority in my life than God's approval. And assuming that rejection was inevitable led me to live my life from a closed, defensive position. Jesus said the greatest commandment is to "'love the Lord your God with all your heart and with all your soul and with all your mind.' . . . And the second is like it: 'Love your neighbor as yourself'" (Matt. 22:37, 39). I couldn't do that with a heart closed off to others.

I loved people's approval far more than I loved God. I built my worth on the shifting sands of whether people liked me, and if they didn't like me, then I didn't like myself. This mindset prevented me from living out these two commandments. God and I had work to do. He knocked on the secret vault deep inside my heart, where I hid all my hurts from rejection and didn't let anyone in to peruse the fallout. Eventually, I could resist his knocks no more; I opened the vault and let him in.

In my home, there is a room—actually, it's an open area with a closet at the top of a staircase. The closet stays somewhat organized, but the room itself has no real purpose. At one point, I envisioned it as a library with a cozy reading nook. But instead, it's the place where the things I don't know what to do with live. So it is with unmet expectations, disappointments, and hurts. When we don't address them and instead roll them over and over in our minds, we eventually tuck them deep into our hearts, where they pile up like the stuff in my wannabe library and spill out into other rooms when there's no place else for them to go.

God helped me pry open the door to the messy room in my heart where the pain from rejection—real and imagined—lived. And he gradually cleared it out, bit by bit, hurt by hurt. One of the first ways he did this was through a Scripture verse, Proverbs 11:27: "Whoever seeks good finds favor, but evil comes to one who searches for it." My experience with rejection and how I handled it led me to live life expecting others to dismiss and hurt me. I needed to begin looking for the good. Instead, my default pattern was to (1) fear rejection and so pursue approval from other people and (2) reject those who dismissed me. Living life on defense puts us in a position of expecting prickles and quills from others, which makes us full of prickles and quills too—anything but tenderness toward others.

Tenderness with each other is a by-product of a life changed by Jesus Christ, but certain habits and thought patterns stand in the way of this demeanor. We nurture our hurts, making our hearts hard. We pick at scabs, reopening them and never allowing a scar to form. Rejection and fear of rejection cut my heart, yet through the work of the Lord, the wounds became healed scars. In his gentleness, God taught me I am already accepted—by him, the only One whose opinion really matters. Once accepted by him, I was free to accept others.

It's out of my sacred scars from rejection that I've learned to be tender and embrace others. By putting God in his proper place in my life and making his opinion my number one pursuit, I learned to stop seeing people as potential weapons designed to inflict harm. Instead, I see them as people whose hearts long for someone to be tender and accepting toward them too. I do not own the market on brokenness. This world is shattered. People are fractured and tear down others with a look or a word or an action, sometimes intentionally, oftentimes not even deliberately. People are in different stages of healing and at various points of spiritual maturity.

Once I stopped looking at my rejection wounds through the lens of "poor me" and started using the lens from Proverbs 11:27, I began to experience healing. Once I realized I was already accepted, I stopped worrying so much about my trials and began to see the trials other people were going through. The wounds became sacred scars and served as a reminder of how much damage rejection creates. That motivates me to present a tender heart, offering love and compassion toward the woundedness in others. And in coming to the realization that I am already accepted by my heavenly Father, I can extend acceptance to others who so desperately long for it.

Working for Acceptance, Expecting Rejection

Have you ever gone against your convictions just to be seen as accommodating? Have you ever gossiped, hoping you would come out looking like the better person? Have you ever silently communicated your assent because disagreeing put you at risk of rejection? These are all ways of looking for acceptance from people not worthy to give it.

In our limited experience and understanding of things of the divine, it's almost second nature to attribute human traits to God. So if people are harsh or cruel, we expect God to be also. Since people judge, criticize, and reject others because of their imperfections, we anticipate judgment, criticism, and rejection from God. It's just one step further down a slippery slope to assume that our painful experiences in life are punishments from God and therefore rejection from him as well.

Many of us pursue people or performance to fill a hole in our heart that can only be filled by Jesus. For much of my young adult life, I exhausted myself trying to be and do all that I thought would secure the acceptance, validation, and approval from others I so desperately craved because I didn't experience it when I was growing up. I endeared myself to teachers by offering to grade their papers or wash their blackboards. I lunged headlong into academic pursuits to compensate for my lack of athletic prowess. Every time someone from church asked me to do something, I said yes so as not to let them down. When patients called in crisis, I bent the boundaries of healthy office hours rather than ensuring I tended to my own emotional well-being. The examples are limitless, but the resulting situational acceptance and validation wasn't. I likely couldn't have described the root of such behavior to you then, but in my rearview mirror of life, I can see I was striving for the thing I never felt I had in childhood: acceptance. I wasn't taught in church that God loves and accepts his children; instead, I learned to view him as a harsh critic and judge just waiting for me to mess up before slamming the gavel and declaring, "guilty!"

The enemy often attempts, as he did with Eve in their initial interaction in Genesis, to convince us that we aren't acceptable as we are; he convinces us that we must do or become something else to be acceptable and accepted. But God says our faith makes us acceptable. "By faith we have been made acceptable to God. And now, thanks to our Lord Jesus Christ, we have peace with God" (Rom. 5:1 CEV). Striving is inconsistent with peace. If we must strive to gain someone's approval, we sacrifice our peace on the altar of acceptance.

Many of us pursue people or performance to fill a hole in our heart that can only be filled by Jesus.

Some will never accept us: we're too little or too much, we're too bold or too quiet, we're too dry or too silly, we're in style or we aren't. Everyone has a different rubric in their head for how they determine another's acceptability. But God already determined long ago that our faith in him, which requires no striving, has made us accepted in his sight.

Expecting Rejection, Finding Acceptance

In eleven short verses in the book of John, we learn of another woman searching for acceptance who had fallen into a painful path of sin. She was subsequently shunned, objectified, and rejected by those around her because of her painful past. John 8:3–11 recounts the battle wounds of this woman, caught in adultery and brought to Jesus by legalistic busybodies hoping to make a spectacle of her and trap Jesus into proclaiming her judgment. From the beginning, the situation reeks of one-sided blame and condemnation. Only the woman caught in adultery was brought before Jesus, while the adulterous man was not paraded or held accountable for his part.

Jesus rarely behaved the way others hoped or expected. He taught in parables, he answered questions by asking questions, and he refused to fall for people's traps, knowing their true hearts and answering the questions they most needed answered but rarely asked. When the accusers demanded that Jesus determine if the woman's offense was punishable by stoning or not, Jesus pointed to the condition of their hearts rather than painfully lodging guilt and shame in the woman's heart. "Let any one of you who is without sin be the first to throw a stone at her" (John 8:7).

The men wanted this woman cast out, discarded, and made a spectacle for all to see. Jesus didn't put the woman on trial. He didn't ask her to confirm or deny her sinful behavior. His behavior was consistent with John 3:17, "For God did not send his Son into the world to condemn the world, but to save the world through him." Rather than reciting all the woman's faults, failures, and insecurities, he bent down and began writing in the sand. We don't know for sure what he wrote in the sand, but I wonder if, in the first instance when he bent down and wrote in the sand, maybe he was listing all the things the accusatory men had done that would bring about shame, guilt, and embarrassment on them if others knew. After he offered them the opportunity to cast the first stone at her, he again stooped down and continued writing in the sand as the men one by one walked away. It makes me wonder if, this time, he wrote all the other nondisparaging things he knew to be true about her (and about you and me) that her sin (and ours) couldn't change:

"You are loved" (see John 3:16).

"You are chosen" (see 1 Pet. 2:9).

"You are forgiven" (see 1 John 1:9).

"You are delivered" (see Ps. 34:4).

"You are accepted" (see Rom. 15:7).

"You are approved" (see 2 Tim. 2:15).

"You are seen" (see Ps. 33:18).

"You are heard" (see 1 John 5:14).

"You are sanctified" (see 1 Thess. 5:23).

"You are renewed" (see Col. 3:10).

"You are redeemed" (see Eph. 1:7).

"You are secure" (see John 10:28).

Accepted and Adopted

When others choose to reject someone, they do so with little understanding of their true motives. Whether we are talking about bullying, criticizing, or completely ostracizing someone else, it usually happens to make the perpetrator feel better about themselves. This was never God's way. "I now realize how true it is that God does not show favoritism but accepts from every nation the one who fears him and does what is right" (Acts 10:34–35).

Many strive to prove to themselves, others, and God that they are worthy of acceptance; in my earlier years, this described me also. We have a Savior who has already declared us accepted without us doing anything to earn it; he has already accepted us and has adopted us into his family, "to the praise of the glory of His grace, by which He made us accepted in the Beloved" (Eph. 1:6 NKJV). In his perfect love, Christ declared that we are already accepted by him, and in dying on the cross to pay for our sins, he made us acceptable to God.

A Scarred Perspective

What then shall we say to these things? If God is for us, who can be against us? (Rom. 8:31 ESV)

My Prayer for You

Father, we all long to know that we are accepted. Help this dear one know that they are forever and always accepted by you, irrespective of their past pain, brokenness, sin, mistakes, or circumstances. Because of Jesus's sacrifice on the cross, we have been accepted and found righteous in your sight. Help them to turn a deaf ear to the lies of the enemy that tell them all they aren't, and let your voice telling them all they are be the only voice they hear. In Jesus's name, amen.

Recommended Playlist

"Wanted," Danny Gokey, © 2019 by Danny Gokey, under exclusive license to Capitol CMG, Inc.

"Broken People," Israel & New Breed, © 2021 by District 11

"Weary Traveler," Jordan St. Cyr, © 2021 by BEC Recordings

"My Future," Ginny Owens, © 2020 by Chick Power Music

"Miracle in Me," Red Rocks Worship, © 2023 by Provident Label Group, LLC

ELEVEN

Scars Reflect Faith, Endurance, and Perseverance

Not only so, but we also glory in our sufferings, because we know that suffering produces perseverance; perseverance, character; and character, hope.

Romans 5:3–4

God wired most mothers to be steadfastly loyal, fiercely protective, caring to our core. Almost nothing will awaken the mama bear in us like watching someone threaten our cubs. An often difficult aspect of parenthood is surrendering our children into our God's care, knowing we can't control them or what happens to them, especially once they interact with the world outside our protective den. Most mothers possess an instinct to protect our cubs even at the risk of our own safety and lives. Parenting is a test of endurance, perseverance, and surrender.

I've worked with thousands of families throughout my career. Many have sought my care and counsel trying to protect their children from physical and medical harm, harm from educational institutions, harm from peers, and even self-induced harm due to immature, misguided ideologies of what they thought was best for them or, at the very least, believed would not hurt them.

From the time they are born, we hold our children close, in our hearts and in our arms, attempting to protect them from the big, bad world outside the relative safety of our walls. Something happens, however, in most families when our cubs approach the precipice of adulthood. Parents understandably begin to loosen the reins while their teens begin assuming greater responsibility for their behavior and any associated consequences. We'd like to keep them bubble-wrapped in their rooms until their brains are fully developed, but that would only engender greater rebellion on their part. During what surely seems like overnight, our children flex their independence, leaving us with wanting, empty arms, petitioning God to protect them from the world's evil.

Motherhood meanders through both the mountain highs and valley lows. I can think of no greater pain in the motherhood journey than that of losing your child to death. Whether through illness, accident, suicide, or at the hands of another, the painful grief mothers endure when their children precede them in death cannot be compared to any other loss. Many times, our children's scars bleed into ours.

Irene, the first friend we made upon moving to Texas, has a "connector" personality: she brings new people into the fold and ensures the underdogs are not only seen and acknowledged but cheered for. We and Irene have experienced the highest of highs and lowest of lows throughout our twenty-five-plus-year friendship: divorce, cancer (for several of us), weddings, book launches, and the devastating loss of her young adult children.

Her scars are sacred and reflect great faith and perseverance in the face of a mother's worst nightmare. Here's her sacred story:

A go-getter from a young age, Irene learned her trade from her parents, who had immigrated to the United States to escape the war in their country. She learned from them how to work hard but honestly and provide for her family, which is how we came to know her when we enlisted her professional services to help decorate our new home.

Irene grew up attending church and took her children to church, but the gospel competed with the alluring evil in the world: drugs, sex, money. She experienced the wreckage from drug and alcohol abuse within her original nuclear family but found it infinitely more painful to realize her own child had not only been provided illegal substances by multiple families in the community but also taught how to weigh and sell them for profit . . . the very thing that would claim her eldest's life at twenty years of age. A mere six years after the death of her first child to a drug overdose, Irene received another call—this time that her youngest child had been involved in an altercation resulting in his death.

Through the nightmare of losing both her children, Irene became furious with God and so desperately wanted the pain to end that she wanted him to let her die to escape it. She found it difficult to praise and worship a God who would do this to her . . . until she came to the realization years later that God didn't do this to her or her children— Satan did. The very one who seeks to steal, kill, and destroy (see John 10:10) had stolen her children from her, killed them, and destroyed the opportunity for her to enjoy life with them. Though the pain, loss, grief, and devastation made it difficult, she determined not to blame or hate God but to persevere in rightfully directing that anger and hatred to the enemy of her soul.

None of us knows how we would handle such great loss and despair until we are in that situation. Irene didn't stay down or let it break her spirit. She pursued God, she persevered, she did what was necessary to deepen her faith, she looked for the real source of blame, and she determined not to let it rob her of joy for the rest of her life. No small order.

We usually react to crises according to what we believed before they hit. Irene grew up in the church, learned about God, and had committed his Word to memory as a child. Her faith was in the saving grace of Jesus. That was her foundation when her children died. She admitted, and I share her sentiment, that "I don't know how people cope when they don't know God." Despite all that the enemy has stolen from Irene, she has determined to find joy in other people's lives rather than continue to harbor bitterness, resentment, and anger over missing out on such joyous occasions in her own life. She walks daily with God, spends time in his Word, and perseveres through life with sacred scars, because she knows he still has a purpose and a plan for her life.

I know of no one today who relates better to troubled teens and young adults than Irene. They gravitate toward her. They love her. They confide in her—sometimes things she'd rather not hear. She speaks into their lives in a way that most cannot, meeting wayward youth everywhere she goes, befriending them and mentoring them. They look to her when they would be loath to listen to another adult authority figure. God has used her sacred scars to speak into the lives of others who are still here and in need of the unconditional love, acceptance, and guidance that she lavishes upon them.

Irene's scars reflect a journey of faith, endurance, and perseverance when Satan wanted her to give up, give in, and end it all. Satan wanted her to be angry with God and rebel against him, turning her back on him. Yet I hear of her daily Bible reading, know of her regular attendance at Bible study, and see her worship at church each weekend. Because she persevered through the most unthinkable tragedies, her sacred scars reveal a work of God's redemption in allowing the very thing that caused her so much pain to be the catalyst for her understanding, empathy, and acceptance of others because she can identify the real enemy at work.

Friend, this is a testament to God's greatest desire for us. When we read that God works everything for our good (see Rom. 8:28), we often think (and hope) that this means he fixes every situation and wraps it up with a pretty bow, like a Hallmark movie. Often, working things for our good means drawing us closer to him and deepening our faith in him even as the threads of our peculiar circumstance continue to lay tangled and knotted, un-bow-like. When pain assaults us, we have a choice about how we will respond. We can either give up and give in, or we can take hold of our Savior's hand and not let go until we're safely on the other side, even if a bit battered and bruised from the battle. There is no greater lifeline than remaining tethered to God and persevering through hard circumstances to gain a stronger, more intimate relationship with him.

Youthful Determination

Tenacity, endurance, and perseverance are born out of great pain and suffering. But they are both a mindset and a choice, as Paul exhorts when he says, "I press on toward the goal to win the prize for which God has called me heavenward in Christ Jesus" (Phil. 3:14). These character traits are innate for some but can also be modeled, as they were for me. Born and raised in New Zealand, my mother possessed spunk and determination. In the early 1960s, she longed to leave her little island in the Pacific and explore the wonder of the world before pursuing love, marriage, and a more settled lifestyle. She was the ultimate introvert albeit with a somewhat determined, adventurous, persistent spirit. She worked two jobs in her native country, saving her wages to secure a passport and fund a transoceanic trip. I imagine my grandmother's and aunt's angst at their youngest daughter and only sister leaving the relative safety of home to travel to places they'd only read about in books or seen in movies.

She set out on her journey, made a friend on the ship sailing to her first stop, and found not only a place to sleep but a job she worked until she could afford to move on to the next country on her itinerary. At one point along her journey around the world, she worked as a waitress in a café in Heidelberg, Germany. A group of young enlisted United States Army soldiers descended upon the café for their evening meal their last night in Germany. In that brief encounter, a young army sergeant struck up a conversation with my mother, making enough of an impression that she shared her address, and they began corresponding between his home in Michigan and wherever her travels led her. Her trip took a detour when they became smitten and he proposed. She moved to Canada until she was able to secure the necessary visa to marry him and live in the United States.

Tenacity, endurance, and perseverance are born out of great pain and suffering.

As a mother who shakes her head when my young adult boys engage in somewhat risk-taking behavior, I imagine the doubts, concerns, fears, and questions my New Zealand relatives had when they learned that my mother was marrying a man from a country halfway around the world and moving there, never again to call New Zealand home. My mother's tenacious spirit was part of her core. God put that in her and caused her to flourish as she pursued a real estate license, became a certified decorative artist, and earned the status of a master gardener.

Difficult Determination

While one could say that perseverance is easier when we're pursuing something fun or interesting like hobbies or vocations, my mother's choices to tenaciously endure and persevere were put to the test in many unpleasant and painful circumstances.

Moving to another country was a difficult adjustment for her. Then when I, her only child at the time, had just turned three and was struck with the deadly illness that doctors were sure would take my life or forever cognitively and physically incapacitate me, my mother determined to prove them wrong. Even though she was not particularly comfortable driving the US roads, she drove me across the state monthly to the University of Michigan's medical center for doctor visits and therapy appointments.

When I required significant reconstructive surgery at the Alfred I. duPont Children's Institute as a young teen, my much younger brother stayed home in my father's care while my mother drove us across the country, where I spent the entire summer in the hospital and she in a boarding house. When doctors cleared me for discharge in a full-body cast, my mother drove all day, with nobody to spell her for a moment's rest, so we could arrive home in time for my brother's tenth-birthday dinner. Neither of us knew when we kissed my father goodnight that evening that he would transition to his home in heaven after his second massive heart attack in two years. My mother's resolve, endurance, and perseverance were tested yet again as she navigated life as a widow and single mother, all while living around the world from her native home, family, and support system.

My mother died young from the ravages of cancer. She and my stepfather were in the process of selling their home, packing, and moving to be near my husband, toddler son, and me when she suffered a pulmonary embolism secondary to her cancer and died. While I miss her terribly, and I pray she would have been proud of me, I'm grateful for the time I had with her here. She taught me about Jesus, about working hard, about pushing through and never giving up, and about pursuing my dreams. I saw many of the scars she carried and knew that she had not lived on easy street. I also knew that she continued to pursue a deeper relationship with her Creator despite and during those difficult times, giving me a battle plan to work from.

Perseverance Exemplified

A lifetime of physical deformity coupled with bone deterioration and surgical scarring resulted in months, years, and now decades of chronic pain for me. Having endured pain, I've felt a kindred spirit in Hannah (see 1 Sam. 1 and 2). When I've endured pain and suffering, I've longed for a hand to hold so I would feel less alone: someone a bit further along in their journey to look to for understanding. Perhaps you can relate. Hannah loved and was loved by her husband, Elkanah, but God had closed Hannah's womb, making her unable to have children, while Elkanah's other wife, Peninnah, was quite fertile and tended to rub it in Hannah's face. Hannah prayed fervently for a child. Every time I read the account of Hannah, her story grabs my heart in a warm embrace that doesn't let go and beckons me to hold on, press in, and not give up on God—for his plans are good and his timing is perfect.

This woman knew suffering. While we don't know for certain, it's quite possible she endured physical pain, as well as emotional, relational, social, and possibly spiritual pain in her barrenness. Without children, which were marks of status and belonging in that culture, she likely felt inferior to Peninnah, who used Hannah's lower status to provoke and taunt her. Though she suffered and others rejected her, her tenacity in the face of rejection and desperation have encouraged me to pursue God with as much zeal as she displayed. Hannah continually offered God her prayerful requests for a son, and every year she accompanied Elkanah to Shiloh, where they worshiped and sacrificed to God.

One year, Hannah prayed in faith, asking God for a son and respectfully and humbly promising that if God would give her one, she would give her son back to the Lord to serve him (see 1 Sam. 1:11). While Hannah prayed silently, her lips moved, and Eli, the priest in the tabernacle, thought she was drunk. She quickly explained, "Not so, my lord . . . I am a woman who is deeply troubled. I have not been drinking wine or beer; I was pouring out my soul to the LORD" (1 Sam. 1:15).

Upon perceiving Hannah's petition to the Lord, Eli told Hannah to go in peace. Hannah left with a change in her countenance, no longer sad, and resumed eating and drinking following her period of prayer and fasting (see 1 Sam. 1:17–18). She left there believing God would answer her prayers.

Oh, how she must have despaired during her barren years. In our humanness, pain often prompts us to question God, to question his plans and his purposes, to question his character. *If I hurt, is God still good?* Did she ask the questions so many of us ask? *God, do you see me? Do you care, God? If you love me, why haven't you healed me? Will I ever receive my healing? Are you done with me, God?* Friend, maybe you've asked some of those same questions in your dark moments of pain and heartache. Don't despair. God's ways and timing are perfect. But what do we do while we're waiting, as Hannah did, for days, weeks, months, or years? Hannah maintained her faith in God and persevered in prayer, worship, and praise, and so shall we.

More Than Physical Healing

In healing Hannah and opening her womb to carry a child, God gave her gifts she may not have even known she needed: he saw her, he bestowed on her the new identity of "mother," he comforted her with the gift of peace that came after she exemplified great faith, and he offered her a future and a return to the social acceptance she had lost. God is often equally if not more concerned about our less obvious emotional, relational, and spiritual healing than our physical healing because they are necessary for us to understand him and his character on a more intimate level. While my husband desired physical healing, God brought him into a closer relationship with him.

After Samuel was born, Hannah fulfilled her promise to God and presented Samuel to Eli the priest and dedicated him to the Lord (see 1 Sam. 1:27–28). This was a great sacrifice by a mother to give back her long-awaited child to God. Every year Hannah returned to Shiloh to worship God, and she brought Samuel a new robe. She and Elkanah were in turn blessed by Eli (see 1 Sam. 2:20). As God so often does, he did more than Hannah asked or imagined and gave her three additional sons and two daughters, which brought joy to her heart, and he made Samuel a judge and a leader of the nation of Israel. Just as Hannah continued to plead to the Lord for her heart's greatest desire, Jesus pleads on our behalf to the heavenly Father, regardless of the sin, the shame, the regret, the pain we possess. He lends his support, strength, wisdom, and intercession when we need it. He recognizes us, calls us his own, offers us worth, and opens the door to the throne room of heaven. He remains our Helper, Adviser, Counselor, and Intercessor.

Thousands of years later, we are inspired by Hannah's prayer, her faith, and her perseverance; we know her because of the painful trial she endured. We may feel anonymous, unnamed, or unknown . . . pained, scarred, and discarded, and yet God calls us his own. Hannah was known not only for her pain but also for how God rewarded her commitment to him and her perseverance in pain. I've often struggled because I don't want to be known for my pain or suffering but instead want people to see Jesus in me through the painful trials. Perhaps you've been referred to, or have labeled yourself, by your pain: the infertile woman, the divorced man, the widow or widower, the woman who got an abortion, the mom whose child has special needs, the couple whose relationship holds scars from pornography addiction, and so on. Those labels may identify the pain you've suffered, but they aren't your identity—your identity is secure as a child of the Most High God.

I haven't always been grateful for pain at the time I've endured it, yet I've consistently been grateful afterward for the lessons learned because of it. God has assured us, "For our light and momentary troubles are achieving for us an eternal glory that far outweighs them all" (2 Cor. 4:17). I'm sure in the case of Hannah, as well as for Irene and my mother (and probably for you), the circumstances didn't feel temporary or easy. Pain and suffering rarely *feel* light or momentary, but when contrasted with the vastness of eternity set before us, the

> **We may feel anonymous, unnamed, or unknown, pained, scarred, and discarded, and yet God calls us his own.**

temporary nature of our earthly pain is put into perspective, while our scars reflect a wound healed by God in his perfect way and his perfect time. The healing process allows us to learn more about God's character so that when we come through the painful trials, we are closer to him than before our suffering, and we have the hope that comes from perseverance.

A Scarred Perspective

Blessed is the one who perseveres under trial because, having stood the test, that person will receive the crown of life that the Lord has promised to those who love him. (James 1:12)

˜˜˚ My Prayer for You ˜˚˜

Father, when despair and discouragement cloud our vision, help us to place our faith in you. Jesus didn't give up, and we have his DNA, so help us not to give up either. Help us to hold on in faith, persevere knowing you aren't done yet, and trust you with the outcome. And when we've done everything we know to do, help us to stand and wait expectantly for you. In Jesus's name, amen.

˜˜˚ Recommended Playlist ˜˚˜

"Carry On," Our Atlantic Roots, © 2019 by Mac Johnston

"Tears," Phillips, Craig & Dean, © 2020 by Gaither Music Group, LLC

"Hold On," Katy Nichole, © 2023 by Centricity Music

"Roses," Andrew Ripp, © 2021 by Andrew Ripp Music

"Open," LO Worship, © 2022 by LO Worship, exclusively distributed by Integrity Music

TWELVE

Scars Remind Us
What Jesus Did for Us

"See my hands and my feet, that it is I myself. Touch me, and see. For a spirit does not have flesh and bones as you see that I have." And when he had said this, he showed them his hands and his feet.

Luke 24:39–40 ESV

Do you have any physical scars on your body? Most likely you remember exactly how those scars came to be and where you were at the time. I have a scar above my left elbow from preschool immunizations. I have scars blotting multiple places on my legs from childhood surgeries, and I have the accompanying emotional scars. I have stretch marks from childbirth. I also bear physical and emotional scars from when cancer was surgically removed; their mere presence reminds me of the day I was initiated into a "club" I never wanted to join. A tiny, white, not-quite-round scar on the back of my right hand reminds me of rushing to prepare to host a friend's baby shower and burning my hand on a hot oven rack. Both the scars and the memories of the sights, smells, and sounds of these moments remain.

I previously viewed my scars with disdain, like my body had betrayed me. Over time, the Lord gently corrected me, showing me that scars are actually evidence of healing, of a trauma that damaged the body, mind, or soul but has since been repaired. Many of our physical scars we now view as trivial, but we didn't at the time the injury occurred. And we have injuries now that are still in the process of healing, many of them nonphysical and not visible. Healing from those internal wounds can be a battle because, unlike the autonomous process that our body uses to heal physical wounds, internal emotional, relational, and spiritual wounds take conscious mental and emotional effort to heal. Battle scars are the tattoos of God's healing touch on our lives. If we will challenge our perspective, they can be a beautiful reminder of what God has done for us and how he has brought us through the pain of our past to the healing in our present. Beauty is in the eye of the beholder, and God deems us beautiful, sacred scars and all. "How beautiful you are, my darling! Oh, how beautiful!" (Song of Songs 1:15).

Battle scars are the tattoos of God's healing touch on our lives. If we will challenge our perspective, they can be a beautiful reminder of what God has done for us and how he has brought us through the pain of our past to the healing in our present.

Frequently, in our pain and our grief we try to make things make sense when, without insight from God, they just won't. Why would God allow a baby to be abandoned? Why would he allow a car accident to claim the life of a parent, leaving their children without? Why hasn't God healed my loved one of cancer? How often in our pain, in our grief, in our hurt do we wonder, *Who are you, Lord, that you would leave me to suffer alone? That you would be quiet when I need to hear from you? That you would heal others but not yet answer my prayer for healing?* How often in our pain do we fail to recognize God in the landscape of our suffering and consequent healing journey?

Too Good to Be True?

Those closest to Jesus undoubtedly had their set of questions too: Why did Jesus have to die? Why didn't he take himself down off the cross? Where did they take him? Jesus's most faithful friends and followers were left without answers to any of their questions for three long, grief-filled days, waiting, mourning, wondering.

When Jesus initially appeared to the disciples after his resurrection, they were afraid and doubtful. To prove he was who he said he was and had done what he said he would do, he showed them his scars from his crucifixion. "He said to them, 'Why are you troubled, and why do doubts rise in your minds? Look at my hands and my feet. It is I myself! Touch me and see'" (Luke 24:38–39). Friends, there have been times I've longed to see those scars, to remind myself that he cared so much for me that he would die so I don't have to. When I think upon his pain, suffering, and death on my behalf, my own pain and suffering pale in comparison.

Thomas missed the first of Jesus's appearances to his disciples, and he was understandably skeptical of their report of Jesus's resurrection. Thomas had pain and scars too. One of his dearest friends was murdered. He grieved; he mourned his loss. He likely questioned what it meant for him and all the other faithful followers of Christ who would now be subject to the Romans coming after them. Thomas had an allegiance to Jesus, and he was asking for assurance that the man who appeared to his friends was really Jesus. Jesus didn't rebuke or chastise Thomas for his doubt. He lovingly provided what Thomas needed in that moment to strengthen his faith.

When Jesus appeared to all the disciples later, he specifically directed his attention to Thomas. "Then he said to Thomas, 'Put your finger here; see my hands. Reach out your hand and put it into my side. Stop doubting and believe'" (John 20:27). In that brief interaction, Jesus not only affirmed his identity but also confirmed that he had done what he promised he would do. Jesus offered Thomas and the disciples the gift of his presence as well as the evidence of his tangible scars so that they would have the assurance to go forward preaching and teaching about him. In that short exchange in which Jesus told Thomas to touch his healed scars, Thomas's grief, mourning, and doubt were healed, leaving him with a valuable testimony to share with future believers.

Doubt, Grief, and Redeeming Scars

Jesus's scars represent a healed wound of his own: the pain of knowing he must die and pay the penalty of our sins because we never could. His scars provide a testimony of his experience. Jesus's sacred scars from his time on earth embody his great love for us. They reflect the extremes to which God was willing to go so that we could be afforded a way for our sin debt to be canceled and for us to spend eternity with him. In his infinite wisdom, God knew that many would need to see Jesus's scars to put their trust in him and believe that he sacrificed his life on their behalf. His sacred scars reflect the healing that took place between the crucifixion and the resurrection and are a crucial part of the landscape of his story.

Jesus's scars prove he can sympathize with our suffering and heal us too. When we look to Jesus's scars, he offers healing for our shame, guilt, regret, and despair. "God made him who had no sin to be sin for us, so that in him we might become the righteousness of God" (2 Cor. 5:21). Because of Jesus's scars, God looks upon us through the lens of Jesus's righteousness, with arms beckoning us to receive his tender embrace of forgiveness, love, grace, and mercy.

Friend, God never wastes our pain. But when we're in the trenches, trying to bandage our wounds and shield ourselves from further injury, we can't see the good that will come as he heals us. During those times, we may have to borrow the hope of others and put our faith in the truth of God's Word. Sometimes Romans 8:28 gets thrown around a little too casually and we cheapen its significance, but we can take God at his word. He will bring beauty from the pain of our ashes, and when our wounds transform into healed scars, we can look back with fresh perspective and gratitude for what he has done. But in the waiting, we are challenged to continue trusting and praising God. We may not praise him *for* the pain, but we can praise him despite the pain, knowing that he *is* working things together for our good, even when we can't yet see it.

Transformative Scars

Sometimes God's provision is comfort. Other times strength. It's almost always accompanied by redemption. It's who he is. Regardless of the gifts he provides in the process of healing our bodies, minds, or souls, our sacred scars serve as a reminder of what Jesus endured for us. I wonder if that was part of the reason God never took the thorn from Paul's flesh—it served as a reminder that despite Paul's pain, God provided exactly what he knew Paul needed.

Therefore, in order to keep me from becoming conceited, I was given a thorn in my flesh, a messenger of Satan, to torment me. Three times I pleaded with the Lord to take it away from me. But he said to me, "My grace is sufficient for you, for my power is made perfect in weakness." Therefore I will boast all the more gladly about my weaknesses, so that Christ's power may rest on me. (2 Cor. 12:7–9)

Sometimes when I read Scripture, I ponder the things we *aren't* told between the pages. We aren't told what the thorn was, but perhaps God intentionally let Scripture be vague to allow us to imagine and insert the source of our own affliction in Paul's narrative to relate to his desperation, his longing, his questioning, his conclusions, and God's provision.

When I think of pain, suffering, mistakes, and misdeeds, the apostle Paul comes to mind. He was a devout Jew who prioritized the letter of the Jewish law and believed in God but, as a Pharisee, didn't believe Jesus was the Messiah prophesied in the Old Testament. He spent much of his early life persecuting Christians for their faith in Jesus. Jews, including men, women, and children, worshiping Jesus the Messiah in local synagogues were his usual target. They endured ostracism, flogging, and persecution to the point of death at his hands.

Sometimes our painful wounds are the result of the behavior of others, but frequently our wounds come from our own decisions or blunders. When this is the case, we experience not only grief and loss but our own personal guilt, shame, and regret. Sometimes our sin propagates immeasurable pain.

Paul's conversion from a persecutor of Christians to one of the faith's most passionate advocates provides a platform for God to use as a testimony of the transformative power of Jesus Christ. It reflects what Jesus accomplished in and through a surrendered life. I can only imagine how much more intently people listened to Paul as he shared the gospel of Jesus as the Messiah because Paul had exhibited such a dramatic transformation after his Damascus Road conversion. How could a man who had previously punished Christians now testify about grace and redemption and become the punished? Paul's life reflected a 180-degree about-face from the life of Saul, as he was previously known.

Hopeful Scars

Friend, we find hope in the chronicles of Paul's story in that if God could redeem a persecutor, a murderer, a villain, a man who set out to destroy the church, he can redeem and use us too, scars and all. He's just that good. Paul's scars reveal that it is possible for God to forgive us and help us learn from our sacred scars while leaving our painful past behind. We all have parts of our past that we'd like to stuff in a box in the attic or throw in a weekend bonfire, never to be seen again. "For all have sinned and fall short of the glory of God" (Rom. 3:23). But God sees, understands, loves, and uses us despite our mistakes, failures, and brokenness as he forgives and redeems.

God isn't going to wrestle us for the reins of our life, but given that Jesus transformed the life of a villainous murderer, we can rest knowing that we are not too far gone for Jesus to step in, forgive our sins, comfort us in our brokenness, heal our pain, and transform our story. He makes our scars glorious. Just as he did with Saul, God knows our potential, even when all we see is the pain or failure that comprises our story. God doesn't wait for us to clean up our act before receiving us as his own and setting us on a new path! God accepts, receives, and loves the Saul in us even before he shows us the Paul inside of us. "But God demonstrates his own love for us in this: While we were still sinners, Christ died for us" (Rom. 5:8).

You might ask, "How can this be? How can God make glorious this shameful wreck of my life?" Let me turn the question around. How many times do we see someone in Scripture asking or thinking essentially the same question? This was Sarah's question when God promised a child from her barren geriatric body. This was the question before Jesus healed and raised others from the dead. Most significantly, this was the question when Jesus was dead and buried, before he walked out of the tomb.

We think of redemption as a onetime event that connects us to God through this incomparable work Jesus accomplished on the cross. God's redemptive work in our lives, though, never stops. He continues to connect us to him in new and stronger ways relationally, emotionally, cognitively, and eventually physically. That which was previously broken is now today being made whole.

Long-Suffering Scars

I don't know about you, but in my darkest, most painful valleys, I've begged God to take my pain away. I've pleaded with him to bring good from bad circumstances. Even as I've written this book, I've asked for supernatural periods of respite from the pain so I could do what I know was his purpose for me to do. And often that prayer has been answered with either a *no* or a *not yet*. For me, that is perhaps the hardest part of suffering: knowing God can right a wrong, heal a hurt, and redeem our mistakes but often not seeing that at work with our own eyes in our suffering. It often comes later, or perhaps in the pages of eternity. When I'm tempted to question and complain about my pain and suffering—feeling certain my better good includes God's healing touch upon my body, my mind and emotions, my relationships, my finances, or even my relationship with

him—I'm reminded of Paul's great suffering *after* he became
a believer and a devout follower of Jesus.

In my own experience with pain in all its manifestations
(physical, emotional, spiritual, relational, financial, and secondary pain, as well as grief), I've had what I considered justifiable
reasons for God to heal me, and I wonder if they might mirror
the reasons Paul may have given God when he begged for the
thorn to be removed:

- "Lord, I could be more productive and do so much
  more for you if I weren't in pain."
- "Lord, you would receive glory from healing me."
- "Lord, I could minister to many more people if pain
  didn't thwart my days."

Paul concluded that God didn't remove his thorn to ensure
that Paul wouldn't become boastful. I can relate. Maybe you
can too. In all transparency, if I lived a pain-free life, or if I
had been able to heal myself each time I required it, I wouldn't
have the depth or breadth of relationship I treasure with God.
As difficult as the painful trials have been from my early childhood through my middle to later adult years, had I not gone
through the pain, I likely would have boasted—at least in my
mind—that I could handle life by myself without the need of a
Savior and a God who redeems. Each period of adversity drew
me back to him, asking for direction, comfort, and healing and
allowing me to experience him in a deeper way as I came to
appreciate more fully my dependence on him.

We know that "we can make our plans, but the LORD deter-
mines our steps" (Prov. 16:9 NLT). And we know that God's
perfect will trumps our human perspective: "'For my thoughts
are not your thoughts, neither are your ways my ways,' declares
the LORD" (Isa. 55: 8). While we desire healing, God desires

that we grow in our relationship with him and that our heart, and thus our resulting character, will bear a greater reflection of him. "The LORD does not look at the things people look at. People look at the outward appearance, but the LORD looks at the heart" (1 Sam. 16:7). So, while we are pain-averse and generally have the elimination of pain as our primary goal, God is more concerned about deepening our relationship with and our dependence on him, growing us to reflect more of his image to the world around us. In my pain, I yearned for relief and physical healing, while God's desire was to teach me more about himself, just as he did with Job and Paul.

While Paul desired the removal of the thorn, God's gift to him was greater and not only impacted the rest of his life but served as a lesson to us as well. The story of Paul's experience with the thorn in his flesh tells us that we must first continually pray and tell God our needs but then recognize God's greater wisdom, timing, and purpose, all delivered in his unfailing, abundant, and indescribable love. Pain always serves a purpose in our lives, and for some, it may serve to underscore our complete dependency on God so that we don't mistakenly assume we can navigate this life on our own. Furthermore, when we deem our painful circumstances too difficult for us, we have access to God's sufficient grace to endure moment by moment and day by day. God does not show disdain toward our weakness—he uses it as a prime opportunity to demonstrate his sufficiency in our lack, his working in our waiting, and his redemption in our pain. Our suffering demonstrates not only that we

> **God does not show disdain toward our weakness—he uses it as a prime opportunity to demonstrate his sufficiency in our lack, his working in our waiting, and his redemption in our pain.**

158

are weak but also that dependence on God offers us strength when it's not otherwise humanly possible to endure. When I am transparent about my pain and suffering with others, I hope they focus not on my feebleness but on the strength and joy of Jesus, which allow me to persevere despite weakness. Paul learned that bragging about his own abilities or revelations was fruitless but that boasting in the Lord would teach others about God and his character.

I identify with Paul's pleading multiple times, asking God to remove the source of his affliction. Sometimes God does, but sometimes he allows our pain to persist even as a greater healing takes place as he reveals to us more of who he is and what he has done on our behalf. God didn't remove the thorn from Paul's side, but he impressed upon Paul the depth of his dependence on God so that Paul didn't become proud in his own abilities. Friend, sometimes God gives us more of what we need instead of just what we want.

A Scarred Perspective

Yet it was our weaknesses he carried;
    it was our sorrows that weighed him down. . . .
But he was pierced for our rebellion,
    crushed for our sins.
He was beaten so we could be whole.
    He was whipped so we could be healed.
    (Isa. 53:4–5 NLT)

My Prayer for You

Father, thank you for what Jesus did on our behalf. Let those reading these words now draw closer to you in thanksgiving for what you have already done, even as they wait upon you for a greater measure of love, comfort, and healing. Never let us forget Jesus's sacrifices to ensure we could have a pain-free eternity. In Jesus's name, amen.

Recommended Playlist

"Scars in Heaven," Casting Crowns, © 2021 by Provident Label Group, LLC

"Nail Scarred Hands," Dante Bowe, © 2022 by Bethel Music

"Mercy Has Won," Kendrian Dueck, © 2019 by Kendrian & Lauren Alexandria Dueck

"Take It to Jesus," Anna Golden and Kari Jobe, © 2022 by Capitol CMG, Inc.

"Jesus with You," FOUNT, © 2023 by The Harmony Group, LLC

THIRTEEN

Be the Gift You Wish You'd Had

> Praise be to the God and Father of our Lord Jesus Christ . . . who comforts us in all our troubles, so that we can comfort those in any trouble with the comfort we ourselves receive from God.
>
> 2 Corinthians 1:3–4

God often uses those painful trials that we think are unique to us to comfort those who also believe their situation is unique to them. "There is nothing new under the sun" (see Eccles. 1:9); this includes our pain. Many will try to lessen their pain, their despair, their complaint with comments such as, "This doesn't compare to the pain you endure." But friend, pain is pain. Whether it comes from a physical wound, a mistake we've made, a friend's betrayal, a child's poor choices, feeling separated from God, or something else, battle wounds cause pain. We process our experiences differently, but the desire for the pain to end and for good to come out of it remains the same. The human heart is searching for redemption, something to make it "worth it."

A Hand to Hold

In your times of greatest pain and desperation, did you long for a hand to hold or someone from whom to seek advice who had already traveled the road you were on? When I endured severe clinical depression, I wanted an empathic fellow sojourner to advise me in my suffering and help guide my journey to healing. That's why I wrote *Hope Prevails: Insights from a Doctor's Personal Journey through Depression*. I wrote the book I wished I'd had when I walked through that dark, hopeless valley because I didn't want anyone else to voyage through that darkness alone.

I also felt the same way when my husband was diagnosed with rare abdominal cancer—we longed for someone to talk to (who had survived) who could encourage us on the hard days and offer helpful suggestions for what to do or what to avoid. While we didn't have that, God used our experience to spur my heart to provide that for others who received cancer diagnoses. A little encouragement ministry was birthed in which we sent cards, texts, emails, or care packages sporadically to remind them that they weren't alone, even as the chemotherapy chairs felt cold and isolating.

> Those who can relate on a personal level to our suffering are often those in the best position to comfort us in our troubles. That's why we can offer that gift to others.

After my husband's treatment concluded and he regained his health, his employer went through a reduction in staff, resulting in his layoff. My husband scoured the paper (we did that back then) looking for appropriate positions, then waited to see if he would be hired. To cope with his sudden change in professional status, he attended a local networking group with others who were in the same position. They shared tips and leads and encouraged each other to stay the course. Their encouragement was the most beneficial because they understood the pain, the discomfort, the loss, and the uncertainty since they had experienced it themselves. Those who can relate on a personal level to our suffering are often those in the best position to comfort us in our troubles. That's why we can offer that gift to others.

The Burden of Aloneness

When I suffered postpartum depression following our first child's birth, I initially didn't recognize it for what it was. I had diagnosed many women with postpartum depression in my private practice, but I had no friends who had admitted to battling it themselves, which led me to believe I should know how to treat it and, sadly, that I deserved to struggle in silence. Only when I began speaking about my battle did other women say, "Me too!"

When I suffered the miscarriage of our second child, again no friends admitted to enduring such an ordeal. I wrestled with shame, guilt, regret, confusion, sadness, grief, and anger without anyone to process it with. I tried to hide my mourning, but the more I attempted to push through and stay busy, the more difficult it became to convince people I was doing fine. I needed to know it wasn't my fault, and second to that, I longed to discover others who had endured similar circumstances and could encourage me.

It's in the waiting, the hurting, the grieving, and the wanting that we crave assurance that someone understands in order to know we aren't alone. When we don't have that, God often seems absent and silent. Scripture reminds us that Jesus is well acquainted with our suffering—he came to earth and experienced pain like we do (see Heb. 4:15), and yet when we endure the battle wounds, we crave evidence of God fighting on our behalf, rescuing us, defending us, comforting us, healing us. Our spiritual eyesight is limited regarding what he is doing in the supernatural, so too often we listen to the lies of the enemy and assume that God is doing nothing.

In some of the hardest battles, people have said to me, "You'll be able to use this to minister to other people." I suspected that was true because I know God doesn't waste our pain. But in full confession, it made me wonder, didn't God care that *I* needed someone to encourage *my* heart? When our pain or our grief is fresh and raw, knowing that our pain will help others with theirs does little to mitigate the hurt, the longing, the disdain, the despair we endure. So, if you are there now, I can relate. For me, it was only *as the wounds healed to sacred scars* that I could appreciate how God used my painful experiences to minister to others, and *then* I was grateful for them . . . helping others somehow gave value to my sacred scars. It gave them a purpose that extended beyond me and was greater than what the enemy had planned for me—a value that lasted beyond my experience.

Childhood wounds are sometimes the most difficult to heal because the effects occur before we understand who we are, before we are grounded in knowing our established identity in Christ, or before we can appreciate how much he loves us. Some of my deepest wounds resulted from childhood events, and it has taken me the longest to appreciate any redeeming value from those, to the point that I stopped looking or anticipating any from some of them. So, imagine my surprise and delight when, in the middle of writing this book, God redeemed some of my greatest pain by using it to encourage and offer hope to another in a similar situation to mine.

The Encouragement of a Shared Journey

A few years ago, a reader messaged me. She had come across a piece I had written and felt that I had been reading her thoughts. My journey through pain, the frustration I had felt with God, and my anger in delayed answers to prayer had resonated with her. But what really spoke to her was my childhood illness and resulting physical deformity and ongoing challenges, which closely mirrored her own life. Through my testimony, she was able to see how God is compassionate and that he sees when we hurt and wants us to come to him for help.

As I said in earlier chapters, I suffered a life-threatening illness as a young child that resulted in significant physical deformity, my petite stature, and unrelenting pain with every step I take. I sport an almost two-inch leg-length difference, scarring all over both legs, and a deformed foot half the size of the other. I underwent so many reconstructive surgeries that we quickly lost count. My physical deformity and limitations were the cause of much childhood bullying. I learned that because I was "different" from my able-bodied peers, they considered me "less than," and I accepted that as the shameful truth. I carried the many physical scars, emotional and relational scars, and the associated shame throughout my childhood and into my adult years. Even today, I consciously choose to cover my legs and feet to avoid drawing unwanted attention to the deformity that scarred my life.

My reader relayed her frustration over a life of pain and unanswered prayers by God, who seemed callous and uncaring. Sometimes, when we have adopted a shame-based mentality, we fear telling God how we feel, but my reader honestly shared her frustration with God during her physically painful journey: "You have authority to change my situation and yet you just stand there waiting." I empathized with the sentiment—how often do we feel that way during our trials? We know God *can* heal and *does* heal, so why doesn't he do that for us?

Our histories were different yet similar enough to offer relatability, as she had detailed enduring many surgeries during a time when children stayed in the hospital alone, propagating the emotional pain of post-traumatic stress disorder. Yet, despite the pain and loneliness, she knew the truth that God still loved her and remained in control.

I never asked God why he allowed this to happen to me; knowing the answer would not be very comforting to me. But I have wondered how God would use my situation for good. Immediately upon receiving this message from a reader, I knew that while my dreadful history fostered compassion and empathy for others, God planned long ago for me to share my story to encourage someone else, and that it did. This knowledge doesn't alleviate the ongoing physical pain, but it brings value to suffering that encourages my heart as much as I hope it encouraged hers. We swapped photos of our sacred scars, grateful that we'd each found someone who could intimately understand the very thing we thought made us so different from others and that God would choose to intersect our lives in such an unexpected way.

God's redemptive purposes for my pain echoed in his purposes for hers. Because she understands the pain that children endure alone, she encourages others who have special needs so they don't feel alone and so they know someone else understands and cares.

Compassionate Scars

While misery loves company, at the root of that is the fact that no one wants to endure painful circumstances in isolation. And we don't have to. We always have the Lord's presence to comfort us in our darkest times, and he hears every cry, including the ones we stifle, trying to remain composed in front of others. But he also comforts us by bringing people across our path who can empathize with our suffering because of their own experiences and weep with us in our sorrow without jumping on the pity bus with us. "Rejoice with those who rejoice; mourn with those who mourn" (Rom. 12:15), or as the New Living Translation puts it, "weep with those who weep." We experience greater compassion for the misfortune of others after we've tasted the bitter root of pain and suffering ourselves. How wonderful that, in knowing what it feels like to walk the lonely path of pain, we can offer our experiences, our hand, our listening ear, our presence to others to spark a bit of light amid their suffering.

When God declared it wasn't good for man to be alone, he gave Adam a helpmate in Eve. Aaron and Hur helped hold up Moses's weary arms. Naomi had the presence and comfort of Ruth. We need people in our lives who will shore up our arms when we're too tired to fight alone anymore and those who will sit with us in our

We experience greater compassion for the misfortune of others after we've tasted the bitter root of pain and suffering ourselves.

pain, loss, and grief, offering unspoken understanding without the common aphorisms or trite phrases that may seem comforting but often communicate a shallow understanding or lack of compassion. When our scars have healed, we become that person for others. Something divine happens when we move our pain over just a smidgen to make room for someone else to have a seat next to us where we can offer support, a listening ear, or a fresh perspective.

We've talked about the enemy inflicting all pain and suffering. God, redeeming all things, takes what the enemy intended to harm us and uses it for good and for his glory. "You intended to harm me, but God intended it for good to accomplish what is now being done, the saving of many lives" (Gen. 50:20). Sometimes he accomplishes that by partnering with us and using our sacred scars to reach down and lend a hand to another who is currently going through their own desolate season. Comforting others with the same comfort we received by investing in them is vital to completing God's healing cycle.

When my pain is all-encompassing, my soul feels dry, my heart is a desert in need of refreshing, and I've lost the joy that I know is promised me, I return to God's instruction through his promises: "The generous will prosper; those who refresh others will themselves be refreshed" (Prov. 11:25 NLT). In blessing others, we are in turn blessed. When we encourage others, we end up encouraged.

When we're clinging to the hem of his garment and longing for our pain to end, however, we often don't *want* to think about others' needs. But God operates in a rather upside-down economy. When I hurt, he desires for me to extend grace to others. When I need a miracle, he calls me to put others' needs before my own and pray for them. When things are tight financially, he still asks that we extend generosity to others. Burdens shared are divided, and joy shared is magnified. From our sacred scars, let's do for others what we wished others would've done for us. I believe with all my heart that God will honor that because it's biblical: "Be generous. . . . Charity yields high returns" (Eccles. 11:1 MSG). In a time of intense pain, maybe that looks like a smile for the clerk at the store or paying for someone's coffee in line behind us or sending an encouraging text to a friend just because. I've found that some of the simplest deeds have the most profound effect when they are done out of selfless love—and even sacrifice—and in turn, they lift our hearts as well.

A Scars Roll Call

Once Leeann learned her identity in Christ and healed from her anger, discouragement, and despair, she was free to be a vessel to offer support and encouragement to other couples. Out of the comfort she received after the end of her first marriage, she now comforts other couples and equips them to heal from their past and move into their future knowing their identity in Christ.

Decades after Lisa endured a violent crime, God healed her heart. She learned that God is her ultimate Protector, Defender, Provider, Comforter, and Healer. Now she uses those insights in her work as a trauma counselor helping others process and heal from their torment. Because of the assault she endured, the sacred scars she bears, and the understanding she has from the perspective of a victim of violent crime, God has endowed her with a voice for those who feel they have none, and she works with legislators to change the laws that currently provide more protection for perpetrators than they do for victims.

In and through his battle with cancer, Scott learned that he needed God to be more than one of the cutout figures used in his childhood Sunday school classes—he needed a personal relationship with him. He benefited from small group Bible study with other men by deepening his relationship with God. And then when that disbanded, he took on the leadership mantle and offered his time and preparation to other men, who have now been studying the Word together for many years.

From her own pain and sacred scars that reflect God's goodness and faithfulness through her traumatic brain injury, Gina impacts others by sharing her story, empathically understanding their experience, and encouraging them not to let their trauma prevent them from being all God created them to be. She uses the pain of her past and her sacred scars to positively impact the younger generation and encourage them to follow hard after the God who spared her life and settled her identity in him.

Pam and her husband, Bill, both came from dysfunctional family backgrounds with poor role models for biblical marriage. They determined to overcome that familial cycle by putting God first in their marriage. They now teach, train, and equip other couples to have solid marriages based on biblical principles through their ministry, Love-Wise.

Often, the truth is buried under layers of shame, lies from the enemy, damaging words from others, trauma, our childhood experiences, or religious rhetoric. Climbing out of the pit of abuse and codependency gave Aliene empathy for other hurting women. Those ashes lit a fire in her soul for every woman to discover God's truth, experience freedom, and live treasured. Jesus said, "Then you will know the truth, and the truth will set you free" (John 8:32), so she founded Treasured Ministries to help women realize the truth as well as discover their voices by turning their hearts toward Jesus and nourishing their souls with the only source of perfect love.

After repeatedly feeling rejected and then, as a reactive defense mechanism, rejecting others, Jessica learned that she was already fully accepted by the only One who matters. God healed her heart, and she adopted tenderness and compassion toward others. Jessica now teaches and writes about viewing rejection through a different lens in order to help others who have suffered rejection's barbs find hope and healing through the Savior who accepts all who come to him.

Irene endured great heartache losing her beloved sons. The enemy wanted her to blame and turn her back on God. Once she realized who the real enemy was, she persevered through and despite the pain, while her faith in God grew. Now she speaks into the hearts and minds of troubled youth, sharing God's love for them through her.

God doesn't call all of us who have endured great pain and loss to lead Bible studies, write books, start ministries, or speak from stages. But he never wastes our pain, and he partners with those who are willing and surrendered to share out of the overflow of their heart after he has brought healing to them as well as sacred scars to honor the battle they've fought. That can be all of us. An encouraging word, a knowing smile, an unexpected card in the mail, a gentle hug can all go a long way in extending a hand to someone in pain to let them know, just as I have tried to do in the pages of this book, that they are not alone and that someone understands or at least cares. Let's thumb our noses at the enemy and give our painful pasts purpose by using them to comfort and encourage others and just see if that doesn't encourage our hearts also.

A Scarred Perspective

For the LORD comforts his people
   and will have compassion on his afflicted ones.
   (Isa. 49:13)

My Prayer for You

Father, for the one still processing and healing from their pain, extend your comfort as no one else can. You sympathize with our suffering. Let them appreciate that in a real and tangible way. And for the one who now bears the sacred scars that testify to the healing they received, help them press into using that pain for good and comforting others out of the comfort you gave. Give them an extra measure of your blessing for being obedient to your Word. In Jesus's name, amen.

Recommended Playlist

"My Story, Your Glory," Matthew West, © 2022 by Story House Music

"Never Walk Alone," Hope Darst, © 2023 by Hope Darst

Book Study Questions

Introduction

1. Before starting to read *Sacred Scars*, what preconceived notions did you have about the purpose of our painful past experiences?

2. In terms of pain (physical, emotional, relational, financial, or spiritual pain, grief, or loss), where are you now in the cycle: experiencing pain, just coming out of a painful trial, or walking alongside someone going through a painful experience?

3. The author pointed out that you have survived every single difficult circumstance in your life, one hundred percent of the time. Where have you previously experienced God's faithfulness?

4. How have you seen God "shape your scars and shape you in the process"?

5. What do you think the author's purpose was in writing this book and sharing her story and the stories of others?

Chapter 1: The Stories Our Scars Tell

1. What do you think lessens trauma, pain, and the feeling of loss over time?

2. Why do we often find it easier to extend mercy and grace to others who have made mistakes or gone through painful trials than to ourselves?

3. How has pain in your past changed you for the better or for the worse?

4. How has God used painful events as a platform or as preparation to draw you to him?

Chapter 2: Scars Signify a Battle

1. What kind of innate reaction do you have to the scars of your past, whether they are physical, emotional, relational, or otherwise?

2. It is possible to experience both pain and joy simultaneously. How have you seen the goodness of the Lord even amid your suffering?

3. In what ways can you look at your scars as "the tapestry of the lessons you've learned through pain"? What has your pain taught you?

4. When you go through painful circumstances, do you tend to focus on the "giant" or on God as your "Giant Slayer," and why?

5. What have you experienced that you still struggle to see any redeeming value in? (If you're not comfortable sharing specifics, at least consider which area those experiences fall in: your health, your relationships, your finances, your walk with God, or something else.)

Chapter 3: Shame OFF You—You Are Not Your Past

1. How has the enemy used shame to demean you or even to attempt to separate you from others or from God?
2. Which one of the ways to recognize shame mentioned in the chapter could you relate to most, and why?
3. How has the pain from your past, whether self-inflicted or not, colored your perception of who you are today?
4. Which one of the statements regarding God's perspective of you do you most need to remember right now? Why is it so impactful?

Chapter 4: Feel It to Heal It

1. In what ways have you attempted to forget your pain and lock it up, like Lisa did in this chapter?
2. We live in a pain-averse society, and if we can't remove our pain, we often try to numb it. What painful experience do you need to allow yourself to feel in order to heal it?
3. How have you endured painful times when you've longed for God to bring justice for mistreatment?
4. Jeremiah went through great suffering yet learned to take his discouragement to God. When have you taken your discouragement to God, and what was the result? Or, if you are feeling discouraged now, how will you give that discouragement to him?

Chapter 5: Scars Can Deepen Our Walk with God

1. As much as we despise pain, it can deepen our walk with God. How have you experienced this to be true?

2. Sometimes in our pain, we are tempted to retreat or isolate from others and from God. How have you experienced God beckoning you to lean into him when you're hurting? What was your response?

3. Frequently we want to know *why* God allows something to happen that hurts us. How would knowing the answer to why mitigate your pain?

4. Which one of the names of God mentioned in the chapter encourages you most right now, and why?

Chapter 6: God Is Good and Faithful

1. What event(s) occurred in your life that dramatically changed the course of it?

2. Read Psalm 102. What encouragement does it bring to your current circumstances?

3. How have you, like Abraham and Sarah, attempted to get ahead of God or "help God out" to try to resolve a painful situation in your own strength?

4. Sometimes we can't see God's goodness and faithfulness when we're in the middle of a difficult circumstance, so it can be helpful to recall previous instances when God has displayed them in our lives. When have you previously experienced God's goodness and faithfulness, and how does that encourage you today?

Chapter 7: We Are Stronger Than Whatever Tried to Hurt Us

1. Sometimes the enemy repeats his tactics from one generation to the next (e.g., addiction, financial destitution, infidelity, etc.). Is this true in your family? If so, how has it played out?

2. What have you endured that has shown you that you are stronger than what tried to hurt you?

3. How have you wrestled with God? What was the result?

4. How has God demonstrated his strength in you so that you weren't dependent on your own limited strength?

Chapter 8: We Are Overcomers

1. When you consider overcoming something, what does that look like to you?

2. How does Jesus's suffering encourage you in your own painful circumstances?

3. Jesus asked God to remove the suffering from him but ultimately surrendered to God's will. When have you had to surrender to God's will rather than your own desires in your painful trials?

4. The lame man's entire identity had to change after Jesus healed him. How has your identity changed after God has healed situations in your life?

Chapter 9: We Are Loved

1. When have you been made to feel that you had to earn someone's love?

2. In this chapter, Aliene shared some of the lies she believed that impacted her understanding of love. What lies have you believed that have impacted what you've thought to be true about God's love?

3. Often, how we've related to our parents impacts how we relate to God. How has that been true in your life?

4. Sometimes how we've been treated in the past impacts our perception of future relationships. How have your

prior relationships positively or negatively impacted how you relate to people today?

Chapter 10: We Are Already Accepted

1. How has your life been touched by the issue of rejection or abandonment? Do you ever find yourself going into new situations anticipating rejection?

2. What have you done in the past in an effort to earn acceptance? How did that work out?

3. The woman caught in adultery expected rejection but found acceptance in Jesus. When have you expected rejection but been met with God's unconditional acceptance?

4. The enemy loves to try to make us believe all the things we aren't (e.g., we aren't good enough, strong enough, courageous enough, etc.). Of all the things mentioned in this chapter that God says you are, which two or three do you most need to receive, and why?

Chapter 11: Scars Reflect Faith, Endurance, and Perseverance

1. The enemy will use our painful circumstances to tempt us to turn away from God. But ultimately, we will choose whether to turn our back on God or run toward him. Which have you done in your pain, and what was the outcome?

2. We all experience hard and painful circumstances. How we choose to endure and persevere through those times makes a big difference. What has sustained you through these difficult ordeals?

3. Hannah persevered in her prayers to the Lord, and ultimately, her prayers were answered. How have you responded when you've prayed and prayed for something but haven't seen God's answer?

4. When we consider the vastness of eternity, we realize that our life and pain on earth are temporary. But it's hard to hold on to that eternal perspective when we're hurting. What helps you persevere when you're tempted to give up?

Chapter 12: Scars Remind Us What Jesus Did for Us

1. What questions have you asked God in the midst of your painful trials?

2. What do you think your response would have been to seeing the resurrected Jesus, complete with his scars?

3. How have you seen God bring beauty from the ashes of your pain?

4. God didn't remove Paul's thorn, yet Paul learned to be content with God's response. How can you learn to be content with God's answer regarding your pain?

Chapter 13: Be the Gift You Wish You'd Had

1. God often uses the painful trials that we think are unique to us to comfort those who also believe their situations are unique to them. When has God used someone else's experience to encourage or comfort you?

2. What experience have you endured that you wish you'd had someone who understood to walk through with you?

3. Joy shared is doubled, while pain shared is divided. Who do you know that you can encourage because of your experience?

4. Scars reflect our *healed* wounds. What scars do you have that God could use to bring hope to someone else who is not yet healed on their journey?

5. How have you witnessed that God never wastes our pain?

Wrap-Up

1. Which parts, if any, of the author's experience or of the other personal stories that were shared in each chapter could you relate to?

2. Are there any passages you marked or would like to revisit?

3. What feelings or emotions did this book evoke for you?

4. Did this book change or challenge any preconceived notions you had about God's purposes for our pain?

5. Which one of the areas of purpose for our pain most surprised you?

6. What is the most important takeaway from this book for you?

7. Who could you recommend this book to?

Additional Resources

- Learn more about Lisa Saruga and both the trauma work and legislative work she does at LisaSaruga.com.
- Learn more about Pam and Bill Farrel and their Love-Wise ministry at Love-Wise.com.
- Learn more about Aliene Thompson and Treasured Ministries, along with their biblical resources to help women heal, at TreasuredMinistries.com.
- Learn more about Jessica Van Roekel's ministry at WelcomeGrace.com.
- Learn more about Dr. Bengtson and her many resources at DrMichelleB.com.

Acknowledgments

How does one adequately say thank you for all the big and little things that offer love, encouragement, and support, effectively holding up my arms like Aaron and Hur did for Moses? For one who loves to craft words, I feel woefully inept at expressing the depth of my gratitude.

Scott, you've always been my biggest supporter, for which I'm grateful. I chuckle at how you patiently endure on the days when I think, "I can't . . . ," and yet you express your belief in me and our God, "Yes, you can." You gladly pitch in and help, whether it's listening to me read a reworded paragraph for the umpteenth time or fixing dinner so I can stay focused. As soon as this manuscript is turned in, I'm looking forward to time for us, even if only to watch the cows roam next door.

This book would not be what it is without the friends who were willing to vulnerably share their experiences, stories, and testimonies of God bringing beauty out of the ashes of their lives to form their sacred scars: Scott, Leeann, Lisa, Pam and Bill, Gina, Aliene, Jessica, and Irene. Thank you for your vulnerability and transparency, which offer each reader hope and encouragement that not only is God not done with their story but he never wastes our pain or our past.

To my former patients who bestowed on me the honor, privilege, and joy of walking with you through your painful journeys: thank you. You taught me about pain, resilience, perseverance, surrender, obedience, healing, and redemption. It is my prayer that you have or will come to see your past pain as sacred scars with a redemptive purpose. If your battle wounds are still raw, it is my hope that you will continue to grow through what you go through and hold on to the truth that God never wastes our pain. You and your sacred scars are beautiful.

Thank you to my fervent prayer supporters and "hard-hat responders." Your prayer support has lifted my arms and lifted my head and appealed to God on my behalf for the strength to complete each task he's set before me. I couldn't do this without you, nor would I want to.

A special thanks to my friend Michelle Sauter Cox, who keeps me chuckling and was the hands and feet of Jesus when she generously stepped in to read an early version of this book and offer her keen insights.

To my beloved agent, Cynthia: you're the best. Sometimes you don't know what you've missed out on until you have it, and that's how I feel about you. I'm so appreciative of your friendship, encouragement, wisdom, insight, writing skills, and effective communication with a smile. I want to be like you when I grow up.

Deep gratitude is extended to the entire Revell team at Baker Publishing Group. Your support, input, wisdom, and guidance make each project better for the collaborative efforts. Thank you for believing in the message of *Sacred Scars* and for working together to get it into the hands of readers. Vicki, I am forever grateful for your belief in me and for championing my work, from pub board to publication. Rachel, I'm so thankful for your sensitive spirit, prayerful heart, and keen editorial skills. I pray we can continue working together for years to come.

Kristin, Holly, Olivia, Brianna, and Eileen, you are the winning team and I'm so blessed to have each of you and your expert contribution to this project. I hope you feel the group hug I'm extending to you.

I'm grateful and blessed to continue writing the words God has given me, yet I'm most blessed by my titles of wife and mom. To my boys: thank you for loving your mom through the painful, hard times, supporting my dreams, and cheering me on. I'm so proud of the godly young men you've become! I will always be your biggest cheerleader.

Most importantly, Jesus, you bore our pain so that we could be victorious in you. Thank you for the scars you bear so that we can recognize purpose in our suffering. Help me to steward my pain well for your glory.

Notes

Chapter 1 The Stories Our Scars Tell

1. Jalen Hurts, "Jalen Hurts 'I Carry My Scars with Me Wherever I Go,'" NBC Sports Philadelphia, December 11, 2022, YouTube video, https://www.youtube.com/watch?v=M1_SlIa2SEQ.

Chapter 2 Scars Signify a Battle

1. Dr. Michelle Bengtson, *The Hem of His Garment: Reaching Out to God When Pain Overwhelms* (Grand Rapids: Revell, 2023), 34.
2. Bengtson, *Hem of His Garment*, 41.

Chapter 3 Shame OFF You—You Are Not Your Past

1. Arlin Cuncic, "The Psychology of Shame," Verywell Mind, medically reviewed by Steven Gans, MD, updated June 28, 2023, https://www.verywellmind.com/what-is-shame-5115076.

Chapter 10 We Are Already Accepted

1. Lecrae Moore, *Unashamed* (Nashville: B&H Publishing Group, 2016), 9.

Dr. Michelle Bengtson is an international speaker, a national and international media resource on mental health, and the bestselling, award-winning author of *Hope Prevails*, the *Hope Prevails Bible Study*, *Today Is Going to Be a Good Day*, *Breaking Anxiety's Grip*, and *The Hem of His Garment*. She is also the host of the award-winning podcast *Your Hope-Filled Perspective*. A board-certified clinical neuropsychologist in private practice for more than twenty years, Dr. Bengtson blogs regularly and offers a wide variety of resources on her website, DrMichelleB.com.

Connect with Michelle

DrMichelleB.com

Ⓕ DrMichelleBengtson   🅲 DrMichelleBengtson

🅾 DrMichelleBengtson   🅟 DrBHopePrevails

🆇 DrMBengtson   ▶ MichelleBengtson

Listen to *Your Hope-Filled Perspective*
on your favorite podcast platform.